Praise for
Starting Over

"*Starting Over* is a remarkable, grace-filled invitation to move past regrets. Dave and Jon Ferguson take us on a journey filled with story and Scripture that guides the reader from a pain-filled past into a positive and redemptive future. This is a life-changing book you need to read and will want to give to others!"

—ANDY STANLEY, senior pastor, North Point Ministries

"Dave and Jon give us the tools we need to find a fresh start! I'm thankful for their wisdom and easy-to-follow steps to freedom."

—MARK BATTERSON, *New York Times* best-selling author of *The Circle Maker;* lead pastor of National Community Church

"Dave and Jon Ferguson's book *Starting Over* will guide you through a healthy, God-inspired process of recognizing, releasing, and redeeming your regrets. Rather than staying in the trenches of the past, it's time to start over and allow God to do a new work in you."

—CRAIG GROESCHEL, pastor of Life.Church; author of *#Struggles: Following Jesus in a Selfie-Centered World*

"The greatest need in human life is a do-over—here it is. I cannot imagine anybody who would not benefit from this book."

—JOHN ORTBERG, senior pastor of Menlo Church; author of *All the Places to Go*

"Dave and Jon Ferguson have built one of the most dynamic and influential churches in America through their passion for telling others about the love of Jesus. Their Spirit-filled energy and vision flows through their book *Starting Over,* with the life-changing message of redemption and grace."

—NICKY GUMBEL, Holy Trinity Brompton

"We all have regrets. Thankfully, we are remi[...] that everything is going to be okay. This book [...]

steps to learn how to be okay and overcome regret. It is an inspiring and compelling message of hope and freedom. Let *Starting Over* be the launching pad for a new season of regret-free living and leading!"

—BRAD LOMENICK, former president of Catalyst; author of *The Catalyst Leader* and *H3 Leadership*

"One of the greatest stories in the Gospels is when John summoned as many who had the courage to the Jordan River. There they could confess their sins and *start life all over again.* John wanted the whole nation to start over because the one to whom he pointed, Jesus, was ushering in a brand new world. *Starting Over* contains the pastoral accounts of one person after another who, like those who entered the Jordan River with John, have learned that God's grace forgives, restores, and ushers one person after another into a life without regrets. What a marvelous book about God's abundant, forgiving, new-life-making love."

—SCOT MCKNIGHT, Julius R. Mantey Professor of New Testament, Northern Seminary

"Regrets are part of the human condition, but how we process them is key to how we will live beyond them. In *Starting Over,* the Ferguson brothers provide insight and tools to help us live beyond regret and into the new opportunities for life and flourishing that God has for each of us."

—DEBRA HIRSCH, author of *Redeeming Sex* and *Untamed*

"I'm not perfect. I've experienced regrets. *Starting Over* provides practical next steps to neither suppress nor forget but rather redeem and release the regrets I've experienced in my life. Unless you're perfect, and none of us are, I think you'll appreciate this opportunity for a new start as well."

—TONY MORGAN, founder and chief strategic officer, The Unstuck Group

"*Starting Over* drives home the message that God has an unending promise of redemption for us. We live in a fallen world and all deal with regrets in this life. . . . Our staff plans to take hold of this tool, and our congregation will experience its impact. I know you will too."

—JOBY MARTIN, lead pastor, The Church of Eleven22

STARTING OVER

STARTING OVER

YOUR LIFE BEYOND REGRETS

DAVE FERGUSON & JON FERGUSON

MULTNOMAH

All Scripture quotations are taken from the Holy Bible, New International Version®, NIV®. Copyright © 1973, 1978, 1984, 2011 by Biblica Inc. ® Used by permission. All rights reserved worldwide. Scripture quotations marked (NASB) are taken from the New American Standard Bible®. Copyright © 1960, 1962, 1963, 1968, 1971, 1972, 1973, 1975, 1977, 1995 by The Lockman Foundation. Used by permission. (www.Lockman.org).

Details and names in some anecdotes and stories have been changed to protect the identities of the persons involved.

Trade Paperback ISBN 978-1-60142-612-3
Hardcover ISBN 978-1-60142-611-6
eBook ISBN 978-1-60142-613-0

Copyright © 2016, 2018 by Dave Ferguson

Cover design by Kelly L. Howard
Interior "Sorry Cycle" graphics by Alex Deeter

Originally published in hardcover and in different form in the United States by Multnomah, an imprint of the Crown Publishing Group, a division of Penguin Random House LLC, New York, in 2016.

MULTNOMAH® and its mountain colophon are registered trademarks of Penguin Random House LLC.

The Library of Congress has cataloged the hardcover edition as follows:
Names: Ferguson, Dave, 1962- author.
Title: Starting over : your life beyond regrets / Dave Ferguson And Jon Ferguson.
Description: First Edition. | Colorado Springs, Colorado : Multnomah, 2016.
Identifiers: LCCN 2016021243 (print) | LCCN 2016025656 (ebook) | ISBN 9781601426116 (hard cover) | ISBN 9781601426130 (electronic)
Subjects: LCSH: Regret—Religious aspects—Christianity.
Classification: LCC BV4509.5 .F4435 2016 (print) | LCC BV4509.5 (ebook) | DDC 248.4—dc23
LC record available at https://lccn.loc.gov/2016021243

Printed in the United States of America
2018—First Trade Paperback Edition

10 9 8 7 6 5 4 3 2 1

SPECIAL SALES
Most Multnomah books are available at special quantity discounts when purchased in bulk by corporations, organizations, and special-interest groups. Custom imprinting or excerpting can also be done to fit special needs. For information, please e-mail specialmarketscms@penguinrandomhouse.com or call 1-800-603-7051.

Unless a man starts afresh about things, he will certainly do nothing effective.

G. K. Chesterton

CONTENTS

In Memory of
Steven John Van Dyke

Nov 19, 1942 - Jan 8, 2012

**God lifted Steven peacefully
up to the angels on the
morning of January 8th.
He was 69.**

Here I am Lord

Is it I Lord?

*I have heard you calling
in the night*

I will go Lord

If you lead me

*I will hold your people
in my heart*

—Dan Schutte

Steve's passions were cars, skiing,
cycling, golf, reading and family.

We will all miss his laughter
wit and warmth.

I've established a webpage to
share Steve's memories and help
fund Pancreatic Cancer research:

lustgarten.org/stevenjohnvandyke

Steven had an aggressive form of pancreatic cancer. Diagnosed on Dec. 6, 2011 as stage 4, it had already compromised his liver. He died five weeks later. We want to help stop this disease by funding research for early diagnosis and treatment.

Help me make a difference. Help us end pancreatic cancer. Visit Steve's webpage to support the Lustgarten Foundation. The Foundation was created to find better treatments and a cure for pancreatic cancer. Your donation will help give pancreatic cancer patients a fighting chance.

— Bonnie

lustgarten.org / stevenjohnvandyke

PREFACE

t's going to be okay.

Soon enough, we'll have some bold things to say to you. But we want to start this book with a gentle, reassuring whisper. And what we want to whisper is this: *It's going to be okay.*

If you've gone to the trouble to pick up (or download) this book called *Starting Over: Your Life Beyond Regrets,* then we're pretty sure it's because an incident, or a series of incidents, is weighing on you and you're unhappy. Something went on in your past that hurts every time you think of it. The idea of starting over sounds incredibly desirable to you, but you're not sure it's possible in your case. And do you want to risk the possibility of more disappointment, more heartache?

If you're feeling this way, we're sorry. And we want you to know it's going to be okay.

While you're going through your painful regret experience, you're far from alone. Researchers say that children as young as nine express regret.[1] Everybody you know who is out of grade school with developed mental faculties has experienced regret and is probably experiencing some of it right now. Regret is an unavoidable consequence of living in this world.

Not surprisingly, the human race has learned a lesson or two about regret along the way. Sages have opined about it. Older generations have passed down wisdom to younger generations on this topic. Artists have produced arresting portrayals of regret. Psychologists have investigated it clinically. The Bible teaches about it directly and indirectly in countless ways.

And now we offer you *Starting Over.* Here, you'll find a clear and practical synthesis of the most important truths that Scripture, science, and story can teach us about beginning again after we've made a mistake or something has gone wrong in our lives. If there's a formula for returning the dawn to our lives, this is it.

The two of us are brothers, and we wrote every bit of this book together. But just so you know, starting with chapter 1, we'll be writing from the perspective of "I," referring to Dave. That's merely for the sake of simplicity. Both of us are speaking to you all the way through.

We are pastors who have not only endured our own regrets, as you have, but have also listened to literally thousands of people tell us about their regrets. An old phrase describes pastors as those who have "the cure of souls" in their care. We have a God-given burden to help the members of our church find the cure for the aches within them. What we've learned from helping them to start over, and starting over ourselves, we now want to share with you via the pages of this book.

So right now we're asking, trust us just a little. Enough to keep reading to see if we can teach you something that will help you start over. Ignore your fear, silence your doubt, and place a bet on the hope you have within you that maybe, just maybe, life can begin anew for you.

The fact is, starting over is not an out-of-reach dream.

It's the way to live your life beyond regrets.

STARTING OVER, STARTING TODAY

CHAPTER 1

THE SORRY CYCLE

Check out these regrets anonymously posted online:

- I regret marrying my husband three weeks ago. I should have called it off before I walked down the aisle. I am twenty-three and just haven't had the time to learn to love myself yet.
- My biggest regret, one that plagues me in my waking moments and some sleeping moments, is that when I was given the opportunity to go to USC for screenwriting I didn't take the chance.
- I regret not telling people how he hurt me. Now, if he is hurting other people, it's my fault.[1]

This stuff is gut wrenching.

And oh so familiar.

Regret is a universal emotion. We all make wrong or foolish choices, or something or someone does something hurtful to us, and we regret it. Sometimes we even start regretting a decision before we make it—because we're so sure the consequences are going to disappoint us!

Some people have bigger regrets or dwell on their regrets more than others do, but everybody has them. So don't feel alone if you look back on some episodes of embarrassing boneheadedness or epic nastiness in your past and wish you could do it again differently.

I wrote this book to help you and many others deal with regrets and start over again. I wrote it for those of us who have ruined relationships, lost jobs, or failed when given golden opportunities. It is for us if we have spent a night in jail, rejected good advice, or hurt somebody we cared about. This is a book for all of us who have regrets of any type burdening our souls and aren't sure how to face the future.

Truthfully, it's for every one of us.

I bet your mind is already simmering with thoughts of your own regrets. They might be minor regrets that you can dismiss from your head whenever you want or major regrets that are painful and crippling and ever present to you. Maybe you even have a mega regret that you try to suppress beneath the surface of your consciousness. It feels like holding down an underwater volcano, doesn't it? Exhausting.

Whatever the magnitude of your regret, and whatever the cause, I have a word of hope for you:

This is not the end.

You don't have to stay stuck in regret.

DIAGNOSIS: REGRET PARALYSIS

Let me tell you how I came to write this book. It started with an observation Jon and I made shortly after the release of our previous book, *Finding Your Way Back to God.*

In that book we described a series of five awakenings that people go through if they feel they have become distant from God and are finding their way back.

1. *Awakening to longing*—"There's got to be more."
2. *Awakening to regret*—"I wish I could start over."
3. *Awakening to help*—"I can't do this on my own."
4. *Awakening to love*—"God loves me deeply after all."
5. *Awakening to life*—"Now this is living!"

In our conversations with people who had read the book, we were pleased that what we had written resonated with so many people. But we noticed something curious: many of the people we talked to experienced the Awakening to Regret but then got stuck there.

For example, one woman in her midthirties told us, "I wish I could start over after my divorce—I really do. But you have no idea how the breakup has affected the way I feel about myself. How lonely I am. What big financial trouble I'm in today. Not to mention the loss of my hopes for having children, which was my biggest dream. Honestly, I don't really see God as caring about me or having anything much good left for me."

Jon and I can't remember which of us first coined the term, but somewhere along the way we started using the phrase *Sorry Cycle* to describe what people meant when they said things like this. They were sorry about what happened and felt sorry for themselves, but they just couldn't seem to get beyond that. Essentially they were going from longing to regret, back to longing then regret, in an endless cycle of repetition.

They were stuck in their regrets.

Paralyzed.

And miserable because of it.

Divorce, abuse, addiction, bankruptcy, the loss of dreams, and other experiences that people go through can be terrible. It's easy to see why so many of us get trapped in sorrow and regret. But getting stuck like this only makes a situation worse. And so we have to be honest about what's really happening here—we have to admit there's a Sorry Cycle in operation.

Psychologists have a term for getting stuck in useless regret: *rumination.* Like a cow chewing its cud, we go over and over our regrets in our mind. That's the Sorry Cycle, and it's destructive. Clinical psychologist Melanie Greenberg, in an article called "The Psychology of Regret," says:

> Regret can have damaging effects on mind and body when it turns into fruitless rumination and self-blame that keeps people from re-engaging with life. This pattern of repetitive, negative, self-focused ruminative thinking is characteristic of depression and may be a cause of this mental health problem as well. . . . Regret can result in chronic stress, negatively affecting hormonal and immune system functioning. Regret impedes the ability to recover from stressful life events by extending their emotional reach for months, years, or lifetimes.[2]

Going round and round in the Sorry Cycle is harmful to our minds and bodies—and I would add our souls to that list too. Furthermore, as we function poorly, the people around us, including our spouses, kids, friends, and coworkers, are forced to deal with a severely damaged person. In a sense, we take them along with us for a ride in the Sorry Cycle.

Sometimes we think that if we try to ignore our regrets they'll shrink over time—or better yet, go away. The opposite is true. Regrets tend to grow over time. And so do their costs. If I neglect my marriage for one month, for example, that is regrettable. But if I neglect it for ten years, the damage will be immeasurably greater.

And then there are the opportunity costs.

Can you imagine the benefits you *aren't* enjoying because you haven't gotten over the failure of your business venture, the rupture in your family, the humiliating public exposure of your immorality, or whatever else you're ruminating about? What peace are you not experiencing? What sense of satisfaction in accomplishment are you missing out on? What connectedness with others are you doing without? What work of creativity are you not able to produce, or what service to the needy are you unequipped to provide? How might your relationship with God be more intimate?

If we don't deal with the roots of our regrets, if we don't make the choice to start over, the costs of what we're missing out on can be enormous and will accrue exponentially over time. Yet sadly, the fact remains that many people, possibly including you, are spinning in the Sorry Cycle today. If left unchecked, anybody's Sorry Cycle can turn into a downward spiral.

A SELF-MADE FAILURE STORY

When I was in my twenties, I knew God was calling me to lead a church. I was desperate to learn how to do that to the best of my ability. And that's why I latched on to Donald.[3]

Donald was the genius behind one of the fastest-growing churches in the country. He wasn't the upfront guy, but everyone close to him knew that he was the leader who put it all together and was responsible for seeing thousands of lives changed.

For that reason, I wrote to Donald and begged him to give me an internship. "I'll do it for free," I said. "I'll get your coffee. Whatever. Just let me hang out with you!" That's how much I wanted to have the opportunity to learn from Donald.

I was thrilled when he said yes to my plea, and I quickly packed my stuff and drove across the country.

The internship turned out to be all I had hoped for and more. Later, I would implement much of what I learned from Donald when I founded Community Christian Church.

I loved and admired my mentor Donald so much.

And that's why I was both stunned and grieved a few years after my internship when I learned that Donald had basically chucked his whole life.

Shockingly, in what seemed like a moment of utter recklessness, he left his wife of twenty years. His explanation was brief and shallow: "We were emotionally disconnected." No doubt there was more to it than that, though I never learned any more details about the causes of the split (nor did I need to). But in any case this marriage was over and Donald's relationship with his two teenage sons would never be the same.

In the midst of all this turmoil, Donald's senior pastor also "suggested" that Donald should resign his ministry position. So that's what he did, begrudgingly. And then, having moved into a small apartment, he lived almost as a recluse for a long time, until he finally got a job as a part-time professor at a community college.

The man who had taught me the importance of relationships was terribly alone.

After hearing what had become of Donald, I called him. On the phone, I thanked him again for all he'd done for me, and he seemed to appreciate that. Then I asked him about how his life was going.

"Are you in touch with any of the old team back at the church?" I asked.

He said no. Then he went on to talk bitterly about the judgment he felt he'd received from some at the church. Eventually, though, he admitted that he had rejected them at least as much as they had rejected him.

"Have you tried to make amends with Barbara?" I asked.

Again, no. The tone of his voice said he wasn't interested in trying to reconcile with his wife.

"What about the boys? What are you doing to restore your relationship with them?"

Here Donald got emotional. I could tell he was in anguish about being estranged from his children. "I've lost them forever," he said.

"But have you *tried* to reconcile with them?" I persisted.

"I did at first, but there's no point in trying anymore," he said. "It's too late."

I hung up the phone that day feeling sad and more than a little confused. I still couldn't understand how this guy whom God had used so powerfully could bail on his family and ministry. Nor could I understand why he was refusing to try to fix some of the mess he had created. He felt badly about what he'd done. But clearly, he wasn't going to do anything about it.

He was stuck so firmly in the Sorry Cycle that he couldn't even imagine a way out of it. And I'm sorry to say that nothing has really changed in the twenty years that have passed since then. As far as I know, Donald has never apologized, never made amends with anyone he hurt, and never truly pursued reconciliation with his family or old friends. He has continued to live a quiet and lonely life with regret seemingly his only companion.

This is what we cannot permit to happen in our lives! And we don't have to. We don't have to get stuck in a Sorry Cycle.

Are you with me?

Next, I want to help you start dealing with your own regrets more productively by helping you understand them better. You see, there are certain

> **Three Types of Regret**
>
> 1. Regrets of action
> 2. Regrets of inaction
> 3. Regrets of reaction

kinds of regrets that cause us to get stuck in the Sorry Cycle. There are three categories that are like giant buckets we can use to start sorting and making sense of our regrets.

WHICH BUCKET IS YOUR REGRET IN?

Every regret is unique, and the sorrow we feel in response to our regrets is deeply personal to us. Yet I've observed that there are three jumbo categories that everybody's regrets fall into. We feel sorry about what we did ("I blew it"), sorry about what we missed out on ("I was too afraid"), or sorry for ourselves ("Why me?"). In other words, we have regrets of *action, inaction,* or *reaction.*

Keep your most painful regrets in mind as you read the descriptions that follow, and see if you can identify which buckets they fall into.

Regrets of Action

The first jumbo category of regrets consists of all those things that make us smack our foreheads whenever we think of them and say, "*Ugh!* I wish I'd never . . ."

I'm talking about:

- Lies we've told
- Relationships we've torpedoed
- Insulting labels we've applied
- Dumb choices we've made
- Rage we've unleashed
- Money we've blown
- Addictions we've fed

Sometimes we have regrets about our actions almost as soon as we've done them. For instance, I know I've said things and instantly wished I could take the words back. Other times it takes us longer to realize the mistakes we've made.

Action regrets constitute the largest and most common category of regrets. Because we make choices many times every day, and because none of us is perfect, we're all vulnerable to regretting what we've done. They might be mere mistakes—errors of judgment or carelessness. Or they might be evil we did knowingly and now we are sorry for it. Either way, they appear in our lives like weeds popping up in a garden and choking out what's beautiful.

Regrets of Inaction

Take a look at this prayer from *The Book of Common Prayer:*

Most merciful God,
we confess that we have sinned against thee
in thought, word, and deed,
by what we have done,
and by what we have left undone.[4]

What we have done: That's action.

What we have left undone: That's inaction.

Often these are referred to as sins of commission and sins of omission. As I've said, the things we regret aren't necessarily sins; sometimes they're just mistakes. Even so, they all weigh heavy on our spirits.

When I refer to regrettable *in*actions, I'm talking about things like:

- Opportunities missed
- Time wasted
- Risks not taken
- Love left unexpressed
- Words not spoken
- Gifts not given
- Forgiveness withheld

Researchers say that, in the short term, people tend to regret actions. In the long term, though, we're likely to regret inaction.[5] It seems that, as we reminisce about our lives, we're prone to wonder about what might have been if we had taken a risk instead of playing it safe.

Older people and the dying, when they look back over a life that seems all too short, often say things like, "My life might have been so much better if I'd gone to college like my parents wanted," or "I wish I'd followed my dream of being an artist instead of just paying the bills as a corporate suit," or "I wish I'd tried harder to work it out with my spouse and never filed those divorce papers," or "What made us so scared about having a child?" or "Why didn't I enjoy life more when I had the chance?"

A poet has said,

For all sad words of tongue or pen,
The saddest are these: "It might have been!"[6]

That's the sound of a regret of inaction.

Regrets of Reaction

Many people, when they evaluate regrets, think only of regrets of action and inaction. But we can't stop there, because sometimes our greatest regrets start with something hurtful that was done to us. Some of these regret reactions come from . . .

- Abuse
- Neglect
- Rejection
- Betrayal
- Mistreatment
- Disability
- Accident
- Illness
- Isolation

When bad things are done to us, quite naturally we regret them. There's nothing wrong with that.

What could be problematic is what we do in response to these regrets. For example, we might assume responsibility that's not ours. *(Maybe there was something I could have done to keep Dad from leaving us.)* Or we might take on shame or blame we don't deserve. *(Maybe if I had dressed differently he wouldn't have touched me like that.)* Or we might stew in bitterness, resentment, and anger. *(I will never forgive the way my brother stole the girlfriend I wanted to marry.)* One way or another, we ruminate unhealthily on our regrets in a Sorry Cycle, and the feelings within us corrode our hearts.

THE GOD LONGING

Whether your biggest regrets are regrets of action, inaction, or reaction, I want you to consider something that might help to explain them all. You see, I believe that all our regrets have a spiritual dynamic underlying them. Specifically, I believe that all of our regrets come directly or indirectly from pursuing longings outside of God.

You might be a follower of Jesus, as I am. Or you might have some different spiritual belief. Maybe you're not even sure God is out there at all. Wherever you are in your spiritual journey, *Starting Over* will give you tools to navigate the road ahead. But even if you don't believe in or are distant from God today, I want you to think about how your regrets might be a part of how a loving God is working in your life for your good.

In *Finding Your Way Back to God,* Jon and I point out that we all have longings for love, purpose, and meaning. As we pursue these God-given longings, we often try to fulfill the longings without God, and that leads to regret. Then that regret leads to more longing, which we again try to fulfill without God, and that brings more regret. Over and over and over we do this. We get stuck cycling between longing and regret.

Let's look at how all three types of regret point us to the true home for our longings—God. As we move from regrets of action, to regrets of inaction, to regrets of reaction, the connection with God may seem progressively more abstract. But in each case, our failure to take our longings to God is the real reason for our sorrow.

The God longing, and regrets of action

It is relatively easy to see how we feel regret when we act on our longings in ways that take us further from God. For example, when we have an affair or click on pornography, rather than turning to God to fulfill our desire to feel loved, we turn to someone or something else—and that leads to regret. Or when we allow our longing for purpose to cause us to become workaholics, that leads to regret. And if we repeat actions like these over and over, we get stuck in a repetition of longing and regret, longing and regret: the Sorry Cycle.

The God longing, and regrets of inaction

This is a little more subtle, but we also feel regret when we don't act on our longings. We long to be loved, but insecurity keeps us paralyzed, preventing us from pursuing a relationship. We long for our lives to have purpose, but fear of failure keeps us from going to college or filling out the application for an interview. The feelings of insecurity and fear that we allow to run our lives do not come from God. And if we give in to them over and over, we again get stuck in a cycle of longing and regret.

The God longing, and regrets of reaction

Our regrets of action and inaction are individual to us. They are about what we did or didn't do. When we get to regrets of reaction, though, we're dealing with hurtful situations caused by other people or by the world. You feel the impact individually, but it can also be communal and global. Yet even here the roots of the problem lie with misplaced longing.

To understand this, we have to go back to the beginning of humankind—theologians look to the story in Genesis 3. Our earliest ancestors sinned, and it has affected everything in a destructive way. What we refer to as the Fall has consequences that we feel to this very day.

The Fall affected every part of us, mentally, emotionally, spiritually. Each person is intellectually limited, meaning we don't know everything and sometimes make ill-advised decisions. Meanwhile, our feelings get tangled up and we don't always know how to react properly to what goes on. Worst of all, we have an inclination toward sin that causes us to act out in wicked ways at times.

All of this explains our evil and foolish decisions and our poor reactions—yours, mine, everybody's. And it's not just individual behavior we're talking about. Our flawed nature also affects our family, the other groups we're a part of, and our society as a whole. If it's human, it's fallen.

Sadly, this gives us innumerable opportunities to hurt each other. People's regrettable actions and inactions affect us every day, often causing us to have counterproductive reactions. And of course we have to admit that we harm others in the same way.

As if that's not enough, the Bible suggests that even nature has been affected by the Fall. In Romans 8:20, the apostle Paul says, "The creation was subjected to frustration." In other words, sin altered a world that God had originally designed to be a safe place for the human race. So if you want an explanation for all the diseases and natural disasters that plague humankind, here is the answer: the Fall.

If we go further in Romans 8, we see that the world has a longing that cannot be satisfied apart from God. Paul says, "We know that the whole creation has been groaning as in the pains of childbirth right up to the present time." And then the next verse explains that this is similar to the individual longing we all feel without God: "Not only so, but we ourselves . . . groan inwardly."[7] There it is—global longing and personal longing. Both are in operation all the time in our lives.

Regrets of action, inaction, and reaction can all be traced back in one way or another to attempts to satisfy longings outside of God. This is good to know, because if there's a spiritual dynamic underlying all our regrets, then there's also a spiritual solution to our regrets. It's in turning toward God that we have the possibility of starting over.

RESTORED TO LIFE

J. R. Ferralez, a middle-aged man with short gray hair and a mustache, sat in the dark on a pier jutting into Lake Michigan, near where he'd parked along Chicago's Lake Shore Drive. He had come to this same spot many times in the weeks since his seventeen-year-old son, Josh, had been killed in an automobile accident. Often he would spend the whole night gazing out over the moonlit waves, remembering, thinking, praying.

J. R. was battling with God. Sometimes he would shout toward the water, as if God were across the waves and might shout back. Sometimes J. R. would swear at God in his anger. Again and again, there were tears.

More than once, people walking by on the pier would ask J. R. if he was okay. He would mutter something to get rid of the well-meaning passersby. He realized they must have thought he was out of his mind.

In a sense, he was.

He was working through a massive and painful reaction to something terrible that had happened. He just couldn't seem to come to terms with his son's death.

With Josh gone from this world, J. R. didn't want to stick around any longer either. Finally he challenged God aloud: "If I jump in, are you gonna save me?" He stripped down to his underwear, left the rest of his clothes on the pier, and jumped into the cold water, immediately starting to swim toward the horizon.

When he got about two hundred yards from shore, he tried to force himself down into the murky water as far as he could go. Twice he did this. He wanted to stay under. He wanted to drown. But he just couldn't physically manage to keep himself down. His body kept bobbing back to the surface, where he would find himself reflexively gasping for breath as he looked out across the lake into the dark sky.

He tried a third time to force himself below the waves and again bobbed up. This time, though, he wasn't facing the darkness. God had turned his face toward the lights of the Chicago skyline.

To the south, he noticed the lights of Soldier Field, where he had watched many games with Josh by his side.

He noticed Grant Park, where they'd attended summer festivals together.

He began remembering good times he'd enjoyed with Josh.

"For the first time since his death," J. R. told me later, "memories came flooding back that brought joy instead of anger and despair. For the first time since my son's death, I wanted to live. I wanted to be there for my wife, and for my other son who was still living, and for my granddaughter."

Fatigued yet hopeful, he began to swim back to the pier and to life.

This grieving father had been stuck spinning in the Sorry Cycle, unable to come to terms with his teenage son's death. Yet even in his case, by turning to God, J. R. broke free. Of course he still grieves for Josh, but he is no longer bound by anger or confusion. He has moved on to a life that is filled with rich relationships, and he is sharing his story to encourage countless others.

If he can break the Sorry Cycle, anyone can.

STOP THE SORRY-GO-ROUND, I WANT TO GET OFF!

For you, this chapter has probably stirred up uncomfortable and specific thoughts of regrets. Let me assure you that you are not doomed to spin forever in the Sorry Cycle over these regrets, any more than J. R. Ferralez was doomed to spin in his.

As long as you're drawing breath, it's never too late to start over. In fact, I'm willing to say:

... no matter what you did or didn't do or what was done to you,

... no matter when it happened,

... no matter how badly it has hurt you,

... no matter how old you are now,

... no matter how hopeless you may feel,

... *it's still possible to start over!*

Although we can't change the past, each of us can have a regret-free life in the future if we will stop looking backward and start moving forward into different ways of believing and behaving. The journey may be a long one. But there's nothing stopping us from taking the first step this very day.

Do you believe that?

Even if you only *want* to believe that, please keep reading.

I'm not appealing merely to your self-interest. I don't want you to be free of the Sorry Cycle and moving ahead in life just so you can be happier (although wouldn't that be nice?). I'm also appealing to you on behalf of the people you love and who love you—people whose lives you can make better when you've broken the power your regrets hold over you. And even more than that, on behalf of all the grace-filled, Spirit-powered things that God still wants to do through you. With God, your future life beyond regret can be amazing!

In the next chapter, I'm going to give you a way of looking at regrets that might seem counterintuitive to you. At first it might even seem crazy. But I believe that as you think about it, you'll begin to agree that this new perspective on regrets has the ability to set you free from the Sorry Cycle.

You can start over, starting today.

No, this is not the end.

This is the beginning.

CHAPTER 2

LOVE YOUR REGRETS

The flickering fire cast light upon the faces of the little group warming themselves around its flames in the still predawn hours.[1] They were waiting in the high priest's courtyard while Caiaphas, inside his house, carried out an unusual overnight interrogation of a prisoner—that troublesome Galilean rabbi, Jesus.

Peter was among the group around the fire, trying to hide from the others how nervous he felt. He wanted to see what would become of Jesus, but he didn't want to get arrested himself and suffer the same fate that he feared his Master was headed for. Twice already he'd denied accusations from people around the fire that he was one of Jesus's group. Despite those self-serving lies, however, he could still feel suspicious glances.

Finally some rough-looking men emerged from a doorway, shoving the prisoner in front of them.

"There's the Galilean," commented a man who had joined the group beside the fire a short time earlier.

"Yeah," said another. "And do you know what? This guy here"—he cocked his head at Peter—"was with him. I'm sure of it. He's got that Galilean accent."

Peter muttered an oath and then exploded, "I don't know what you're talking about!" He would have said more, but just then he heard a sound: the raspy gargle of a rooster crowing.

With that, the realization came to him all in a rush.

He remembered the conversation at dinner the night before. The disciples had been arguing about who was most loyal to Jesus, deserving of a place of privilege by his side. Peter had boasted, "Lord, I am ready to go with you to prison. I'll even die with you!"

Jesus had replied, "Peter, before the rooster crows in the morning, you will deny three times that you even know me."

Peter hadn't believed it at the time. But now he realized he'd done just that—denied Jesus. Exactly three times.

Almost against his will, he turned to look at Jesus standing nearby in the courtyard.

Jesus gazed back at him, staring deep into his eyes. The look was filled with sorrow and love, yet to Peter it felt like a spear piercing his soul.

Isn't that the way it is when we have regrets? We feel pierced with the realization that we've done something wrong or that someone has done something wrong to us. We squirm, but we can't get away from the reality of what's happened. The wound reaches deep into our soul, and who knows how or if it will ever be healed?

For Peter, Jesus's look seemed to confirm his self-accusation. After everything Jesus had done for him, Peter had refused even to be associated with Jesus in his most desperate hour. Peter had acted cowardly. Dishonest. Unfaithful. The shame of it was overwhelming. Everything appeared hopeless to him now.

Without even waiting to see what terrible things the guards had in mind for Jesus, Peter rushed out of the courtyard. As he stumbled through the dark and deserted streets of Jerusalem, convulsive sobs forced themselves from his throat.

What was Peter going to do with his overwhelming regret?

What are we going to do with ours?

REGRET BREAKOUT

Mentally rehearsing our regrets over and over in a Sorry Cycle gets us nowhere. Moreover, it does us a lot of harm. That's what we learned in the previous chapter.

So what *should* we do?

I have some advice that may sound strange: Don't regret your regrets. That's right—*don't regret your regrets!* Learn to love them instead, because they can teach you how to pursue a life you don't need to regret.

I'm not talking about loving that difficult occurrence from your past, trying against all reason to force yourself to be glad about it. Look, if it was tough, it was tough. (I'll say more in the next chapter about the importance of being realistic about your regret.) Regret is usually a highly rational emotion.

I'm talking about loving the fact that you have a strong emotional response to the difficult experience—your sense of regret. This sense of regret can be a useful corrective. It can be your means of moving beyond feeling sorry and starting to create a better life for yourself and those you love most. I call this movement a *regret breakout*.

In one of his letters to Jesus's followers in Corinth, the apostle Paul contrasted "godly sorrow" with "worldly sorrow."[2] The Corinthians had committed some actions that were undeniably regrettable, and when Paul pointed out their error, they felt deeply sorry about it. Paul praised them for this response to his chastisement.

Their sorrow wasn't a worldly sorrow. It didn't consist of being sorry they got caught and then beating themselves up about it, with no good coming out of the experience.

In other words, they didn't get caught in *the Sorry Cycle.*

Instead, it was a godly sorrow, one that led to repentance. That is, they did something about their regret. They went to God asking for forgiveness and seeking from him the power to learn and grow from what had happened. Paul pointed out that this meant they were not harmed by their temporary regret, but rather they were filled with zeal to set things right.

I would say they had a *regret breakout.*

And so can we.

Your Brain on Regret

Did you know that regret is actually visible? It's true. Scientists using advanced neuroimaging technology have taken pictures of people's brains when they are feeling regret, and the scientists have seen the orbitofrontal cortex light up.[3]

Now, here's what I want you to note. The orbitofrontal cortex is a part of the brain that's involved in both reasoning and emotion. So this means regret is not just a vague feeling unconnected to facts or ideas. It's a *cognitive* feeling—an emotion that's tied to specific thoughts. You don't feel regret in general; you feel regret about driving too fast in proximity to a state trooper, or repeating an unfounded rumor, or something else definite and concrete. There is something specific in your mind that has caused your regret. This is what I meant when I said that regret is a rational emotion.

But more than that, let's keep in mind that learning usually works best when thinking and emotions are paired. Strong feelings about the personal relevancy of a topic reinforce the importance of new ideas to us. And so, given the position of regret in the brain, this means that our regret can be the source of personal growth, with feelings and ideas working together to help us learn from the past and make better choices in the future.

I think we sense this intuitively. In fact, according to one psychological report, people identified regret as being the most beneficial of twelve negative emotions under study. The respondents said their regret helped them make sense of past experiences, taught them about themselves, and enabled them to alter their future behavior for the better.[4]

Marcel Zeelenberg and Rik Pieters, a couple of experts in psychology, say, "Regret is an aversive, cognitive emotion that people are motivated to regulate in order to maximize outcomes in the short term and learn maximizing them in the long run." They add that regret is distinct from other emotions because of its behavioral consequences.[5] What these scholars are saying is that regret is an emotion that is both negative and often painful, while at the same time incredibly helpful for our future decision making.

Doesn't that make it easier for you to love your regrets?

In her very popular TED talk, journalist Kathryn Schulz gets blunt on the subject. She says,

> The inability to experience regret is actually one of the diagnostic characteristics of sociopaths. It's also, by the way, characteristic of certain kinds of brain damage. So people who have damage to their orbitofrontal cortex seem to be unable to feel regret in the face of even obviously poor decisions. So if in fact you want to live a life free of regret, there is an option open to you. It's called a lobotomy. But if you want to be fully functional and fully human and fully humane, I think you need to learn to live, not without regret, but with it.

Schulz concludes her talk by saying, "Regret doesn't remind us that we did badly. It reminds us that we know we can do better."[6]

FEEDBACK LOOP VERSUS SORRY CYCLE

Feedback is what happens when the output of a system is routed back as input, forming a circuit. Feedback occurs in many kinds of systems, including electronic systems, biological systems, and even social and emotional systems. Typically, the feedback can be either positive or negative.

The Sorry Cycle is a kind of negative feedback. Through unhealthy rumination, we let our regrets route back to our deeply felt longings in a way that often leads us to make even worse decisions than we did before. The results are about as pleasant to experience as the squeal of a PA system when the sounds coming out of the amp feed back through a microphone.

But regrets don't have to produce negative feedback. If we are mindful of what we are doing with our regrets, we can make different choices that turn those regrets into positive feedback.

What if, instead of merely letting your regrets make you feel dissatisfied and uncomfortable, you faced them squarely and interrogated them, demanding the useful information they can provide? The feedback won't give you everything you need to know about how to make the best possible decisions in the future, but if nothing else, it will surely give you some valuable data about what *not* to do. It's an indispensable starting place for making a change in your life and breaking out of the Sorry Cycle.

And this interrogation is not a one-time operation. Over time, we can continue to consult our regrets for what they can teach us. The feedback will serve as data for fine-tuning our actions and behaviors. This ongoing reevaluation of feedback should result in better consequences.

So think of regret as potentially useful feedback on your life. If a certain action, inaction, or reaction has proved harmful, then you can learn from it and do better next time. It makes a lot of sense to learn to love your regrets; they can be life changing, yielding information that leads to personal growth.

A SELF-FULFILLING HISTORY

Consider this. If you're stuck in regret, maybe the problem is that you're telling yourself a bad story.[7]

You see, when something goes wrong—we did something bad or something bad was done to us—our minds naturally try to make sense of it. We put it into a structure of meaning. In a way, we construct a story about what it means to us.

And that story isn't always good.

Think about these explanatory narratives:

"I hurt my friend so badly that we'll never have a relationship again."

"If I was going to start my own business, I should have done it before I got married and had kids."

24

"I've tried everything to quit smoking, and it's impossible."

These stories tell us we're stuck. We can't get past whatever it is we regret.

And if we tell ourselves a story like that often enough, we come to believe it. Naturally, we don't try to move beyond the place where we are stuck. Why would we? It's not in the script!

Of course we need to see negative events for what they are. We have to be realistic and tell ourselves the truth. But that's different from making assumptions about what an event in the past means for our future. Realism about a regrettable incident, in fact, should include recognizing the limited influence the past has to hold us back. The obstacle may not be as large as we have assumed.

So if the stories we're telling ourselves are too lacking in hope, let's change them—not to try to talk ourselves into something that isn't possible, but to try to open our minds to a genuine possibility. The feedback provided by regret suggests the new story line.

"I hurt my friend badly, but maybe she's ready to forgive me now. I wouldn't be surprised if she misses me as much as I miss her."

"I can't go back and start a business the way I would have before I got married. However, maybe I can follow my entrepreneurial dream now in a way that doesn't put my ability to provide for my family at too much risk."

"It would have been better if I'd never smoked that first cigarette when I was seventeen. But even after years of smoking and numerous failed attempts at quitting, the next time might be the one that succeeds."

The uses we make of the feedback our regret gives us open the possibility that our personal narrative can have a happy ending.

BETTER OFF DEAD

Thirty-one-year-old Brett reached a decision.[8] As soon as he was let out of the mental health ward at the hospital, he would take his own life the first chance he got. It wasn't a question of *if.* It was only a question of *when* and *how.*

Brett was broke and homeless and, in his mind, a hopeless addict. He'd been transferred to the mental health ward after spending a week in the ICU due to a near-fatal heroin overdose. The hospital staff wanted to get him in better shape, mentally as well as physically, so that hopefully he could survive on the outside.

Brett, however, had no such hope. He'd already been through too much as a drug and alcohol addict. He'd made too many failed attempts at sobriety. Now he felt that he had nothing to live for, and he hated the thought of causing his loved ones any more pain. It was time to take the final exit.

Meanwhile, as he looked back on the mess of his life, there was one choice he regretted more than any other, because it was the choice that had started the downward spiral that led him to where he was now.

Five years earlier he was on a business trip and decided to have a drink. After all, he was out of town at a sales conference and that's what you do, right? And besides, he told himself that he could handle alcohol again.

That's where he was wrong.

Back when Brett was a thirteen-year-old, he and a friend had broken into his father's liquor cabinet, setting off a drinking and drug problem that had lasted throughout his teen years. Only when he was in college did he finally get sober. After that, he'd gone on to start a successful career in the mortgage banking industry. When other people his age were struggling with the question, *How can I pay the rent?* he was asking himself, *Should I get the Lexus or the Porsche?* He bought a couple of houses. He got engaged to a wonderful woman named Melinda. He was feeling proud of himself and confident about the future. And so, after logging a few years of sobriety, he convinced himself that he'd moved past the danger that alcohol had once posed in his life. He could not have been more wrong about that.

What the twenty-six-year-old Brett thought would be a harmless drink on a business trip turned out to be the furthest thing from harmless. He kept drinking. At first only when he was out of town. Then on the weekends. Then after work. Then during lunches.

Trying cocaine at a party while drunk led eventually to bloody noses, crack pipes, heroin needles, overdoses, empty bank accounts, and hepatitis C. He was in and out of AA meetings, detox centers, and hospitals. The allure of the addictive substances always won out over the treatments.

Brett remembered, "I worked very hard at staying intoxicated. Partially to keep from feeling sick. However, I think just as strong was the need to not remember all that I had lost and all of the pain I had caused others. Regret was truly the most overwhelming theme in my life."

I asked Brett to identify some of his regrets. It was a long list. Here are a few of the items he mentioned:

- Selling every possession in his home, including the dishwasher, to buy drugs
- The shame of filing for bankruptcy and losing his homes
- The hurt he caused his family as they watched him slowly dying in addiction
- The crushed dreams of his fiancée, Melinda, who lost her wedding and the man she had thought she was going to marry
- Panhandling on the streets so he could buy just one more bag
- Living in ghetto hotels and crack houses with prostitutes and pimps
- Feeling far from God

Crushed by these regrets, waiting to get released from the mental health ward, Brett decided he couldn't live with the hopelessness and regret any longer. It was time to leave this life.

But then, as Brett puts it, God happened.

Gifts from God

Many of the other patients in the mental health ward with Brett had serious mental illnesses. One day one of the women was coloring with a crayon when the crayon broke, causing her to shriek and to cry out that her life was over.

Brett tried to comfort her by saying that it was just a crayon and her life was certainly not over.

In that same moment he heard a whisper of a thought in his head: *It doesn't have to be over for you yet either.*

Brett somehow knew that thought was from God. He didn't see what hope he realistically had, but the message held comfort for him anyway. It was the first glimpse of possibility he'd had for himself in a long while.

After his stint in the mental health ward was over, instead of killing himself as he'd planned, he agreed to go to a rehab center in Florida. Once again, he received help and encouragement to stay sober. The treatment program in itself, however, wasn't the turning point for him. The turning point came in an unexpected moment afterward.

Following his discharge from the thirty-day program, Brett was sitting at a bus stop waiting for a bus to take him to a new job as a gas station attendant, where he would make less in a year than he used to make in a month. He was feeling sick from the hepatitis treatments. It was August in South Florida, so the weather was oppressively hot. He couldn't believe how far he'd fallen and what misery he'd endured.

There at the bus stop, he felt angry.

He felt alone.

Then he started crying.

And in that moment God gave him a gift inside the desperation—he was able to let it all go.

"I made a deal with God that day," Brett told me. "I said, 'Okay, God, I'm yours. If this is the best I can look forward to in life, I'm okay with this. If I can't ever do anything more than be a guy who makes people smile for a moment at a gas station, that is enough for me. After all, I don't really deserve more than that.'

"In that painful, sad, raw, and honest moment of letting go of everything, I let 'Brett' die—the 'Brett' I always thought I needed to be. In the death of that 'Brett' I found life. God gave me a new purpose for living."

Brett was learning from the feedback his regret was giving him. By the grace of God, he could now picture the possibility that the rest of his life story could be truly different. This was his breakout moment, and finally he could start his life over again.

He has been sober since that day and has found a new freedom and happiness in living. He's married to Melinda and is the father of two children now. He's making a good living again in the business world, but this time he's not living for himself. His focus is on sharing his own experience of pain and loss and, more importantly, his story of hope with others who are struggling to find a way out of addiction.

Purified Longings

Now I want to return to an idea I have already introduced and build on it.

When I talk about loving your regrets and using them to change your life for the better, I'm not just talking about the practicalities of making better choices. Not that there's anything wrong with making smarter decisions or having wiser judgment about when to take risks and when not to. Starting over has the potential to be so much more.

As Brett's story reveals, starting over isn't just about making a change—it's about making a change *with God*. There's a spiritual dimension to it. And the new life we enter into is not just a better life that we dream for ourselves but the better life that God dreams for us.

If you remember from the previous chapter, the Sorry Cycle is basically about having a longing, trying to fulfill it in an inadequate or harmful way, feeling regret about it, and instead of trying to do something different, attempting to fulfill our longing in a faulty way again. The problem with that approach is that, in the deepest and fullest sense, our longings can only be fulfilled in God, not in seeking to satisfy our own desires.

So as we're trying to use our regrets to move us ahead in life, let's remember what direction we're supposed to be going in: back to God. Always. A better life for us will be one that seeks to know God and love God and follow God.

This makes it possible for me to give you some amazing encouragement:

Even as you are trying to improve your circumstances, God is invisibly at work in your life. It's a joint process, even though you may see only your own side. On God's side, he desires to fulfill your longings and redirect your efforts so that you need not feel regret.

The apostle Paul, prior to following Jesus, lived a life full of regrets that could easily have kept him stuck in the Sorry Cycle. Perhaps because of his own experience, he had some harsh words for those who were turning back to their old ways: "Formerly, when you did not know God, you were slaves to those who by nature are not gods. But now that you know God—or rather are known by God—how is it that you are turning back to those weak and miserable forces? Do you wish to be enslaved by them all over again?"[9]

I love how Paul trips over his own wording: "You know God—or rather are known by God."

We may know God, but if we do, what's more foundational than that fact is that he knows us.

We may believe God, but he initiates our belief.

We may obey God's commands, but he empowers our obedience.

So you're not alone in trying to break out of your Sorry Cycle. God is with you, making it possible by his power and his grace.

Do you remember the story of Peter that we started this chapter with? At the end of it, Peter had just stumbled away from Jesus. He was crushed by regret over having denied his friend and Lord three times.

But because of Jesus's initiative, the story has a beautiful and redemptive sequel.

DAWN IN PETER'S HEART

What a feast it was! Peter had never known another breakfast like it.[10]

The food was ordinary enough—just roasted fish and bread. But the company! Jesus himself had cooked the breakfast, while Peter and some of the other

30

disciples were out fishing on the Sea of Galilee. Now they were all eating together at the shore.

This was the third time Peter had seen Jesus since he had risen from the dead, and yet Peter could still hardly believe the Lord was alive. Peter wanted to laugh every time he thought of it. He and the other disciples were all filled with such awe and happiness. They kept glancing at Jesus and smiling uncontrollably as they talked.

Even the pale-yellow light of dawn as it streamed over the water seemed special. Like this was the first morning of creation.

The only thing that spoiled the moment for Peter was the sting of remorse he felt for having denied Jesus. As much as he wished he could forget what he had done, that was impossible. His fear and faithlessness at that time seemed all the more misplaced to him now, in light of how Jesus had demonstrated his victory over every opponent, including death.

Had Jesus forgotten what Peter had done in Caiaphas's courtyard? They hadn't spoken of it. Peter couldn't believe the incident had passed from Jesus's mind.

So Peter wasn't entirely surprised when the conversation took a turn at the conclusion of their meal. Jesus looked at him and asked, "Peter, would you say that you love me more than these other men?"

The other disciples looked on, curious as to how he would reply.

Peter was ashamed as he remembered his boasts on earlier occasions about being more faithful to Jesus than any of the other disciples. After his denial of Jesus, he could never boast like that again. Yet what was he to say now? He didn't want Jesus to think he didn't love him. He did. Now more than ever!

Finally he replied in simplicity, "Lord, you know that I love you."

Jesus surprised him by what he said next: "Feed my lambs."

That sounded like Jesus wanted him to be a shepherd over Jesus's followers. Could it be that Jesus was going to give him responsibility, even after he had proved he wasn't worthy of it?

Before Peter could ask Jesus to explain his words, Jesus repeated, "Peter, do you love me?"

Jesus had to ask again? This was confusing. Peter didn't know where he stood with Jesus.

The silence this time stretched on for several moments, fraught with tension. In the end, with a trembling voice, Peter said, "Yes, Lord, you know that I do."

Again came the enigmatic command: "Feed my lambs."

Peter said nothing. He waited for it, and it came:

"Peter, do you love me?"

Peter could only insist on his love yet again.

"Then feed my sheep," said Jesus.

Three times? They had to go through all this *three* times?

And then Peter understood.

Just as three times he had denied Jesus in the high priest's courtyard, now here, on the shore of the future, Jesus gives him the opportunity to recommit himself three times. And Jesus readily accepts his promise of faithfulness and love. He even entrusts great responsibility to him.

Out of Peter's regret was birthed a deep love for Jesus and a heartfelt passion for his mission. Even when Jesus went on to warn him that he would one day pay a high price for being faithful, Peter could scarcely contain his elation. The regret that had hovered in the background of his thoughts ever since he had denied Jesus now evaporated like fog struck by sunlight.

It was a new day after all!

LIFE LIVED FORWARD

A Danish philosopher named Søren Kierkegaard once said, "Life can only be understood backwards, but it must be lived forwards." I think you're ready to see regret, not as something to regret, but as something to love because it is priceless feedback that allows you to better understand your life. I also think you're ready to start moving beyond regret—moving forward in the direction God has for your future.

In the next chapter I'm going to begin telling you *how* to use your regrets to make progress. It turns out, there's a three-step process that works for every kind of regret. You're about to discover how to break out of your own Sorry Cycle.

SECTION 2

BREAKING OUT OF THE SORRY CYCLE

CHAPTER 3

STEP #1: RECOGNIZE YOUR REGRETS

O n April 9, 1995, fifty-one-year-old Liverpool engineer Timothy O'Brien looked in his newspaper for the results of Britain's National Lottery. He couldn't believe his eyes. From what he was seeing there, his numbers had come up for the major prize!

O'Brien was half of a two-man partnership of lottery ticket buyers, and he always played the same set of six numbers. As cowinner of the top prize, his takeaway would be worth about £2 million, or more than $3 million. It was the kind of payday he had long dreamed about.

But then O'Brien remembered something. He'd neglected to renew his stake in the partnership, and his numbers had run out on April 1. What a cruel April Fools' Day joke!

A huge regret of inaction set in immediately. O'Brien's response to it was rapid and tragic. This father of two climbed the stairs to his attic, grabbed the handgun he kept there, and shot himself in the head.

There's one more awful irony to the situation. You see, O'Brien hadn't looked at the lottery results carefully enough. Actually, only four of O'Brien's numbers had come up, not all six, so he had missed out on only about £27 (less than $100), not £2 million. For that miscalculated regret he gave up his life.[1]

There are foolish, even tragic ways to react to regret. And then there are helpful, productive ways.

In this chapter and the two that follow, I want to detail a three-step process that can empower you to respond constructively to any type of regret: First, we *recognize* our regrets for what they are.

Next, we *release* them so they can no longer hold us back.

Finally, we trust God to *redeem* our regrets—that is, bring something beautiful out of whatever it is we are feeling sorry about.

The redemption of our regrets is an amazing outcome to contemplate if we have been stuck in the Sorry Cycle, getting nowhere and feeling miserable, perhaps for a long time. The first step in moving toward redemption is to learn to properly recognize our regrets. What, exactly, is it that we are feeling badly about? Have we either underestimated or overestimated how serious it is? What power does it have or not have to affect our future? We need to answer these questions if we want to start over after regret.

As I said in the previous chapter, don't regret your regrets. Love them. Recognize them, feel them, mine them for all they're worth, and then get ready to leave them behind.

> **How to Break Out of the Sorry Cycle**
> 1. Recognize your regrets.
> 2. Release your regrets.
> 3. Redeem your regrets.

That seems like simple advice, doesn't it? Maybe too simple? Yet the human mind has some reflexive responses to powerful emotions such as regret that can make it hard to honestly face reality.

For that reason, I've got two *don'ts* and one *do* for you when it comes to taking stock of your own regrets.

DON'T DWELL ON YOUR REGRETS

When people say things like, "I just can't stop thinking about that rude comment I made to my friend," or "I stay awake at night wondering what would have happened if I'd had the guts to ask her out," or "I go over and over the accident in my mind," they're ruminating on a regret.

Up to a point, mentally rehearsing something regrettable that happened might be helpful to you. If the situation was a big surprise, ruminating can help you overcome the shock and adjust to the new reality. If it was a complicated situation, thinking it through can help you untangle the threads of behaviors and motivations that were involved.

We want to learn from our regrets. So it's good to analyze a regret and try to understand what really happened. I'll be saying more about that before we finish this chapter.

But all too often we go way beyond performing a helpful post-analysis of a regret. We keep replaying our regret in our mind over and over and over again until it takes up far more of our attention than it merits. Instead of helping us, dwelling on our regret is making it all worse. For some of us, in fact, it may not be too much to say that we're torturing ourselves with regret.

This isn't healthy.

It's the opposite of healthy.

I have a friend named Michael who purchased one hundred shares of Amazon stock when it was $83 dollar per share, for a total of $8,300. He was confident in his purchase, even reassuring his skeptical father, "Amazon is the Walmart of the Internet!" But after watching the stock price drop for several reporting periods, Michael lost faith in the investment and decided to sell his stock for $38 per share.

Mere days later, Amazon rolled out the Kindle and the company's stock shot up. Its general trend has been up ever since.

Years later, when I asked Michael about this experience, he commented, "Right now, Amazon's share price is at $573. So I took $8,300 and turned it into $3,800. It could be $57,300 if I'd held on to it. I need to let that go, but it's hard to shake."

Michael is still obviously grinding his teeth about this investment mistake. But ruminating is not putting lost money in his pocket.

If you engage in similar rumination, it isn't going to help you either. Instead, it's going to cause your regret to swell in importance in your mind out of all rational bounds and to seem like a permanent obstacle to a better future, when in fact it is no such thing. It's going to act as fuel to keep the Sorry Cycle spinning. It's circular energy that doesn't do anything for you except make you discouraged.

Author and professor Dallas Willard wrote, "The ultimate freedom we have as human beings is the power to select what we will allow our minds to dwell upon. It is in our thoughts that the first movements toward the renovation of the heart occur. Thoughts are the place where we *can* and *must* begin to change."[2]

Willard is challenging us to apply something the apostle Paul wrote in 2 Corinthians: "We take captive every thought to make it obedient to Christ."[3] To take our thoughts captive is to determine what we will or will not dwell upon. So don't dwell on your regrets too passionately or too long. Take enough time to adjust to your regrets and to gather whatever insights you can get from them, and then flip the lever to turn off the rumination machine in your mind.

Don't Hide from Your Regrets

What may be more dangerous than thinking too much about your regrets is not thinking about them at all. That is a huge mistake! In many ways, we try to ignore or escape from our regrets. We don't face them at all—or at least we don't face them truthfully. Here are three ways we hide from our regrets.

Denial

If you hear these kinds of statements, you know you're in the presence of someone who is in denial about a regret:

From a woman who has alienated her friends and family members with her selfish behavior: "I can't remember ever doing anything wrong to any of them. It was their fault, not mine."

From a husband who has placed virtually all the burden of parenting on his wife: "We each had our role, and mine was to provide for our family."

From someone who is out for revenge after being unfairly criticized by a coworker: "I think I'm justified in trying to stick it to him just like he stuck it to me."

At times each of us attempts to redefine regret or reinvent the truth. We rationalize or minimize our regret or try to talk ourselves out of it entirely. Through the magic of denial—*poof!*—we make it go away. Or at least we pretend we did.

Distraction

Sometimes I wonder how many drinking binges might be due to people trying to drown their regrets. How much weed is smoked, how much meth is injected, how much oxycodone is pilfered from medicine cabinets to distract people from thinking about what went wrong in their lives?

If a man puts a ridiculous number of hours into his job, is he just a workaholic, or is he trying to escape the thoughts of something he regrets?

If a young woman tries to have friends around her all the time, continuously blasts music in her ears, and goes to parties late into the night, might she be trying desperately to keep regret at bay?

It's in solitude and silence that we let memories arise, pray and hear the voice of God, and make decisions. But when thoughts of regrets are too intimidating, we can seek instead to drive them away with whatever means of distraction lie at hand. We may not realize what we are doing, because we want to distract ourselves even from the recognition that we are distracting ourselves!

Suppression

Just as we sometimes change the subject when a conversation becomes uncomfortable to us, so we sometimes change the subject of our inner thoughts. We try to divert or delay our thoughts of regret so we don't have to deal with them. We suppress them, hoping to bury them so deep that we'll never see them again.

Scarlett O'Hara, in *Gone with the Wind,* deals with her regrets over the loss of her antebellum lifestyle by suppressing them. Whenever a painful reminder of her changed circumstances, or the need to make a decision, intrudes into her consciousness, she says something like this: "I can't think about this now! I'll go crazy if I do! I'll think about it tomorrow. . . . After all, tomorrow is another day!"[4] But she keeps pushing "tomorrow" into the future and pushing her regret down below the surface of her consciousness.

Just as dwelling on regrets is natural, so wanting to hide from them is natural too. It's a self-protective response. Who wants to deal with the emotional pain that regret brings? Who wants to go over a seemingly unsolvable problem one more time? Who wants to feel powerless before the impossibility of changing the past? I've got nothing but sympathy for people who feel deep hurt as they consider their regrets.

Furthermore, I'd say that—depending on how we go about it—hiding from our regrets can even be helpful for limited periods of time. For example, temporarily suppressing thoughts about regret can enable us to stay on task with something else that's more urgent at the moment. If we're not able to deal productively with our regrets right now, then setting them aside for a time might make good sense.

But long term, there are a couple of real problems with the strategies we employ to escape or bury our regrets.

The first is that the methods we use to hide from our regrets can be more harmful than the pain we're trying to escape from. Given enough time, denial torpedoes relationships, distraction feeds addictions, and suppression distorts temperament.

The second problem with hiding is that we need to face our regrets sooner or later if we are ever going to get the better of them. Hiding from regret interrupts the helpful feedback loop of information that regret can provide for us. So if we are hiding, we need to have the courage to turn and face the bogeyman of our fears.

In a way, then, it's a good thing that hiding from regrets rarely works for long. We might twist logic into a pretzel to try to convince ourselves of something that isn't true, but our conscience and our fundamental rationality won't let us put up with the self-deception forever.

We might say to ourselves, *Hey, look over here!* and *No, look over there!* in order to keep our attention focused on anything but our regret. But eventually we get weary with the effort and our focus drifts back to what went wrong in our lives.

We might push a regret down below our consciousness, but then it remains in our subconscious like a log that is going to have to bob up to the surface at some point.

A Wolf in Denial

Jordan Belfort—best known for his portrayal in the film *The Wolf of Wall Street*—soared and crashed during the wild decade of the 1980s on Wall Street. At one point his firm, Stratton Oakmont, employed more than one thousand stockbrokers and worked with $1 billion in stock issues. During the entirety of his firm's existence, however, he was under investigation for fraud and money laundering. He was eventually convicted and spent time in prison.

At the end of his run, Belfort's firm was responsible for more than $200 million in losses from the investors for whom he was supposed to be working. Without a second's thought, Belfort would take people's savings and wash them away so he could increase his own wealth. He was court-ordered to pay back more than $110 million of those losses, though he has tried to wiggle his way out of doing that.

It seems that Belfort remains in denial of what he was doing. He said, "Ninety-five percent of the business was legitimate. . . . It was all brokerage firm issues. It was all legitimate, nothing to do with liquidating stocks."[5]

One former member of the SEC has said, "Stratton Oakmont was not a real Wall Street firm, either literally or figuratively."[6]

Ironically, Jordan Belfort is now a motivational speaker. He has apparently not fully embraced the regret of what he's done.

We can't live beyond regrets if we deny them or otherwise try to escape from them. Only when we are willing to really face our regrets and be honest about them can we pull the plug on the power that our regrets have over us.

To illustrate this, I want to tell you about another leader who (with a push from a friend) reacted entirely differently than Belfort to his wrongdoing.

SHEEPISH

The prophet Nathan waited all morning at the back of David's throne room as the king heard petitioners and dispensed justice.[7] "My brother refuses to vacate the vineyard our father left me when he died." "Our Levitical family isn't getting its fair share of the meat and grain from the tabernacle services." "It's true I cannot pay my debts, O king, but can't you help a poor widow keep from selling her son into slavery?"

Nathan had to admit to himself that David was patient with each of the petitioners and showed a real passion for justice. But what would happen when Nathan declared that it was the king himself who had done wrong?

The prophet waited until all the citizens had left. Then he strode across the echoing flagstones of the throne room floor to approach the king.

"You've decided to come up at last, Nathan!" said the handsome middle-aged king with a smile as he rose from his seat and stepped off the throne platform to greet the prophet.

"Aye, king," said Nathan. "Today I've my own tale of injustice to tell."

"Then tell away!" said David.

And Nathan proceeded to implement his strategy.

He knew David's secrets. How lust had boiled up inside the king like some wicked brew when he saw the lovely Bathsheba naked. How David had soon impregnated this woman who belonged to another man. How he had schemed first to deceive and finally to murder Bathsheba's husband—one of David's most loyal and capable soldiers. How, after the murder, David had gone on with his new wife and son as if he had done nothing wrong.

At any point in this process, David's sense of justice should have erupted and caused him to recoil from the evil he was doing. But instead he had made his heart harder at every turn. And now, if he felt any regret at all over his adultery, lying, and murder, that regret lay hidden beneath the hard shell David had built up around it in his soul.

Somehow Nathan had to pierce that shell. And so his plan was to use a simple story, almost like a fable told to children, to get around David's defenses. He said to the listening king,

> There were two men in a certain town, one rich and the other poor. The rich man had a very large number of sheep and cattle, but the poor man had nothing except one little ewe lamb he had bought. He raised it, and it grew up with him and his children. It shared his food, drank from his cup and even slept in his arms. It was like a daughter to him.
>
> Now a traveler came to the rich man, but the rich man refrained from taking one of his own sheep or cattle to prepare a meal for the traveler who had come to him. Instead, he took the ewe lamb that belonged to the poor man and prepared it for the one who had come to him.

As Nathan told the story, he watched David's face and he knew his plan was working. David's expression showed no sign of recognizing that *he* was the rich man in the story, a thief who had stolen a wife from a man who had so much less than David did. Instead of revealing guilt, the king's normally ruddy face had grown dark with righteous anger.

David exploded, "The man who did this deserves to die! Before he's executed, though, he must pay for that lamb four times over, because he had no compassion in his heart."

This was the moment. David was ready to receive what was coming.

Nathan thundered, "You are the man!"

At these words, the king took a step back as if he'd been struck.

Nathan went on to detail the Lord's disgust with David and decision to punish him. And as he did so, the shell inside David cracked. Appropriate feelings of shame and guilt, diligently suppressed until now, flooded his spirit.

Instead of trying to deny what he'd done or making excuses or claiming exemption, he finally faced the awful truth of his transgressions. Hanging his head, he said, "I have sinned against the Lord Yahweh."

His deep-seated regret was at last out in the open for him, for Nathan, for God, and for all the world to see.

Do FACE YOUR REGRETS HEAD-ON

Let me be Nathan to you today. I want to tell you something sternly yet kindly, because it is for your own good.

If you have been dancing around your regrets, trying to pretend they're not there, it's time to stop. Or if you've gone to the other extreme and have given too much power to your regrets, to the point where you can't even see them plainly, you've got to stop that too. It's time to bring all the honesty you can to your regrets, recognizing them for what they are. This prospect might seem intimidating at first, but it's the only way to live beyond your regrets once and for all.

Embrace the truth.

We may think we know our regret all too well—after all, it feels like we've been living intimately with it for a long time! But actually, even though the pain of our regret may be terribly familiar to us, that doesn't mean we've looked at the regret itself as carefully as we need to.

So take time to assess what went wrong in your life. Be as clearheaded as possible about it. Is yours a regret of action, inaction, or reaction? What is the right label for what happened? How big of a deal was it, really? What is its lasting impact?

Perhaps it would help if you thought of this as interviewing yourself about your regret, like a reporter trying to get to the bottom of a story. Try journalism's classic Five Ws and an H:

- Who was involved?
- What happened?
- When did it happen?
- Where did it happen?
- Why did it happen?
- How did it happen?

Beyond the mere facts, what are the effects of the regret? How has the situation affected you mentally, spiritually, and emotionally? Maybe because of what went wrong, you've become a less courageous person, more closed off from the world. Maybe you're drifting from God. Maybe you're depressed.

It's not that I want you to wallow in bad feelings. But it's just as important not to grieve your regrets too little as it is to grieve them too much. Perhaps if David had grieved his lust and lying sooner, he wouldn't have taken the tragic step of murder.

Also be honest about how others might be hurting because of what happened. Particularly if you are responsible for their pain, you need to admit to yourself how you've hurt them. Because then maybe you can do something about it.

Don't shield yourself. You're after the truth, the whole truth, and nothing but the truth.

Take from it what you can.

Business gurus preach that making mistakes and learning from them is a key to having entrepreneurial success in the long run. Military commanders debrief unsuccessful missions to help them plan differently for the next operation. In order to escape the past, we have to mine our experiences for whatever they can teach us.

It's not just about gathering information regarding our regrets; it's also about putting them in perspective so that we know what to do with them. What does your regret teach you about what you need to do more of, do less of, or do differently in the future?

If you're divorced and thinking about remarriage, what can you learn from your first marriage about being a better spouse in your next go-round?

Do you look back and realize that you tend to give up too easily when the going gets tough? How can you hang in there next time?

Could the persistence of your desire to be a playwright mean that God is calling you to try once again to express your creativity in a script?

This process of evaluating your regrets isn't always an easy one. Nor a quick one. Understanding might come progressively and in stages.

I suggest getting alone, praying for God to guide you, and keeping a notebook nearby to write down insights you receive. If emotions overflow, don't be afraid to cry. If you think you would benefit by having someone to talk this over with, enlist your spouse or a good friend. You might even want to make an appointment with a therapist or a spiritual director—a professional who is trained to help others hear the voice of God.

Facing our regrets can be hard work, but the benefits are so worth it.

THE TRANSFORMATION OF A SNAKE

In *Finding Your Way Back to God,* I wrote about my friend Steve Ciambrone.[8] This was a man who built a successful business, married a wonderful woman, and had two great kids and yet came close to completely trashing his life. Later he admitted, "I was chasing women, doing drugs, drinking, lying, cheating, stealing—basically snakelike activity." With the help of some other men, he found his way back to God and experienced a beautiful, authentic relationship with Jesus. But it was too late for his marriage. When he confessed the last affair to his wife, she said she'd had enough and told him to move out of the house.

What I didn't know when I was writing about Steve the last time was that he then had only months to live. He'd been battling cancer off and on for a few years. Suddenly it was on again. And then it was all over.

I spoke at Steve's funeral service. Hundreds of people came to celebrate his life. Steve's ex-wife—the woman he'd repeatedly cheated on—was sitting in the front row. She wanted to be there. His kids, now adults, were there too. They spoke lovingly about their dad at the funeral even though he was the reason their family had split up. Many of Steve's friends and business acquaintances wanted to say good-bye to him too, despite the fact that there were times when he'd been a complete jerk to them.

How could a one-time snake like Steve receive such honor at his death?

I think it's because he recognized his regrets and dealt with them.

There was a time when he refused to take responsibility for his wrongdoing. For example, he blamed others and his unfair circumstances for his alcoholism. "Poor me, poor me, pour me another drink" is the way he described his attitude at the time. He'd essentially made himself a god in his own life, and so whatever he did was right in his eyes. The fault always lay elsewhere.

"It took me a long time to recognize that I wasn't God," Steve said. But he eventually admitted his faults to himself and to God, apologized to those he'd hurt, and made amends wherever he could. The people in his life saw his sincerity. They could also sense the change in him after he found his way back to God. He became a kinder, less self-centered, more responsible person.

For Steve, recognizing his regrets made the difference between dying as a lonely outcast and dying knowing hundreds of people who loved him would be at his funeral.

YOUR CHOICE

You can't change what happened in the past. But, like Steve Ciambrone, you *can* change what you do in response from here on out. Your choice of response is all important for your future.

That's why you have to be brave enough to face your regrets and stare them down until they lose their power over you. When you do that, your regrets won't be a finish line. They'll be a starting line!

Never doubt this: God does not want to leave you crushed under the weight of your regrets. He wants you rescued from your burden. Scripture advises, "Cast all your anxiety on [God] because he cares for you."[9] In the next chapter, we will teach you how to do this. Now that you've recognized your regrets, it's time to release them.

CHAPTER 4

STEP #2: RELEASE YOUR REGRETS

After finishing high school, I enrolled at a Bible college in a small town in Missouri. For a while, things went great for me at this college. I made friends, played on the basketball team, and grew spiritually. The school had strict rules, such as a dress code and a curfew, but I had a lot of fun anyway.

In my junior year, the college hired me as the director of recruitment. I don't know what possessed them to ask me. I don't think they had ever had a student fill that kind of role before, and I'm quite sure they have not since! Nevertheless, I was given an assistant, three part-time staff members, some outreach teams to deploy, and an office next to the president of the college. My brother, Jon, was my right-hand man.

One of the first things we did was to revamp the college visitation days. Breaking tradition, we brought in bands and speakers that the students actually liked. The result? Record numbers of high schoolers showed up for college visitation days. Soon enrollment at the college hit a peak too. All the numbers were up and to the right. I was feeling successful and like I was making a difference—I thought I was exactly where God wanted me.

Then it all imploded.

During my senior year, Jon and I were driving back from a recruiting trip, when we arrived at the college fifteen minutes past the 9:00 p.m. curfew. (Yes, 9:00 p.m.!) Our dorm dad met us at the door and told us he was writing us up. Not only that, but he also informed us that he'd "had enough of us" and that we would be "roomed" as a consequence. We could not leave our rooms except to go to chapel, classes, and meals for the next seven days.

The next day I got a note informing me that Jon, a couple of other friends, and I were to meet with the president of the college. When I walked into the boardroom, to my surprise, there were a bunch of men sitting around the table. The college president and representatives from the college board of directors were all waiting for me.

The president and board immediately began talking about the seriousness of this situation, which, up until this point, I had not taken seriously at all. Next, they listed the many ways in which I had either displayed misconduct or misrepresented the school. These accusations included breaking the college curfew, disobeying the dorm dad, and displaying an overall attitude of arrogance.

Looking back, I realize the school administration didn't like who I was, where I was from, or how I operated. Some of them referred to Jon and me and our friends as "the Chicago gang." (That's not a compliment when you are in rural Missouri.)

I was being unfairly treated. And yet I wasn't without guilt of my own. I'm sure I did come across as arrogant.

At the end of that meeting in the boardroom, the college leaders informed me that they were going to dock me four weeks of pay for my job in recruitment as well as require me to apologize to the entire student body at chapel the next morning.

I went back to my room shaking my head.

What I did next confirms that I thought I was too cool for school—I slept through chapel. When the time came in the chapel schedule for me to make the apology that I had been ordered to deliver, I was conspicuously absent.

Now, I thought (and still think) that the whole "rooming," board meeting, and work-without-pay treatment was absurd. But I certainly didn't help matters by sleeping through chapel!

I was told later that, after my no-show at chapel, the college president made some critical comments about me to the student body.

After that, Jon and I knew we had to leave. In the middle of my senior year, I transferred to another college. I hated leaving my friends. I especially hated leaving under a cloud of apparent disgrace. And I wasn't too happy that I wound up putting in an extra year at college in order to have enough credits to graduate from my new institution. But I had no choice.

I remember kneeling all alone in a prayer room at my new college shortly after arriving there. I asked God, *Why? Why would you allow me to be removed from a place I loved? Why would you take me out of a role where I was making a difference?*

The answers didn't come. At least not immediately. And so I was left with a lot of regret.

But here's what I want you to note: that prayer was the beginning of my releasing my regret. In time I was able to forgive those who had treated me unfairly, forgive myself for making matters worse, and put it all behind me.

QUESTIONS FOR STARTING OVER

When we have done something wrong, or when something undeserved has happened to us, we come face to face with issues of justice and fairness. We can easily get hung up in guilt, blame, and grudge-holding. The questions and emotions inside us can prevent us from moving past our regrets and heading in a new direction for our future.

So I have a word for you . . .

If regret has become a useless burden around your neck, drop it. Let it go. Release it.

Now, what this release looks like depends on what has happened, who's responsible, and how you have reacted to it. If you have practiced the first R and have recognized your regret for what it is (see chapter 3), you should be able to identify the situation you're in when it comes to releasing that regret. I have five questions for you to ask yourself that will show you just what you need to do.

Please take this seriously. In fact, I'd say that if you're not willing to grapple with these questions, you might as well put this book down right now. Without going through the stage of releasing your regrets, you will never really start over.

I'm glad that I wrestled with God's plan in the prayer room of my new college, and you'll be glad you wrestled with the questions of repentance, forgiveness, and release that follow.

Question 1: Do you regret committing a sin?

Sometimes what we regret doing falls into the category of sin. It was not just a failure; it was something you did that disappointed God and put distance between you and him. For example:

- You lost your job and your reputation by stealing from your employer—*a sin of action.*
- You have refused to be generous to people in need—*a sin of inaction.*
- Your mother treats your sister better than she treats you, and as a result, you let anger erupt toward her—*a sin of reaction.*

It's important to determine whether your regret involves sin or not, because if it does, letting go of the regret will require driving around the spiritual roundabout known as repentance and proceeding in a different direction. To repent is to agree with God that you have turned away from him, or have not followed his plan for your life, and to resolve to live differently in the future through his help. If you've sinned, repentance is a critical part of starting over.

But I don't want to leave the impression that repentance is some sort of impersonal religious transaction between you and God, like paying a bill on PayPal. Repentance is fundamentally relational. When you sin, you create distance between yourself and God, and repentance bridges that separation, bringing you back into an intimate relationship with God.

Let me show you what repentance looks like by telling you the sequel to a biblical story we encountered in the previous chapter. Do you remember the episode when the prophet Nathan confronted King David with a story about a lamb?

After delivering God's blistering criticism of David's behavior with Bathsheba, the prophet Nathan turned and walked away, leaving the king alone. In their interview, David had admitted, "I have sinned against the LORD."[1] Now all the pretense of innocence he'd been keeping up was over, and David was left to deal with the aftermath.

It could not have been easy for a man like David to admit that he had caused himself to be on the outs with God. Here was a guy who had been described as a man after God's own heart.[2] He was a warrior who trusted that the battle was the Lord's.[3] He was a lover of God who worshiped with such abandon that it was embarrassing to others.[4] He was the "sweet psalmist of Israel" whose musical talent was exceeded only by his spiritual depth.[5]

And now he stood before God as an exposed adulterer and murderer.

What next?

David did what he had done in moments of distress or other situations of powerful emotion ever since he was a youth. He picked up his harp, headed for a place of solitude, and strummed out his feelings before God.

Thankfully, we have a record of the song he composed at this time. The description for Psalm 51 says, "A psalm of David. When the prophet Nathan came to him after David had committed adultery with Bathsheba."[6] Here we get a glimpse into David's feelings at this juncture in his spiritual life.

I want to point out a couple of lessons we can learn from Psalm 51.

First, David was facing his sin squarely. He had owned his mistakes. He was letting himself feel his regret. And he knew what he needed—forgiveness.

Imagine you hear the strumming of a harp and a tearful voice singing these words:

Wash away all my iniquity
    and cleanse me from my sin.
For I know my transgressions,
    and my sin is always before me.[7]

David had recognized his regrets and was seeking to release them through confession to God.

Second, David was concerned about the future of his relationship with God. With his acute spiritual sensitivity, he understood that his sin was a wedge that had created distance between him and God. Nothing was more painful to him than that separation.

That's why he further sang,

Do not cast me from your presence
　　or take your Holy Spirit from me.
Restore to me the joy of your salvation
　　and grant me a willing spirit, to sustain me.[8]

God did forgive him and restore their relationship. On God's behalf, Nathan assured David, "The LORD has taken away your sin."[9] Tragically, David's son would die (a reminder to us that our sin has consequences even when we repent).[10] Nevertheless, David was able to start over with God and start over in his life.

You may not be a musician or a poet like David, but if you have sinned, creating distance between you and God, then you too need to pour out your honest feelings of sorrow and repentance. Ask God to restore your relationship so you can move forward with him. Don't let pride or embarrassment keep you from taking these necessary steps as soon as possible.

Echo Forgiveness

If you're the kind of person who readily accepts forgiveness and moves on once God has forgiven you, then you can skip to question 2 below. But if you're like most people, including me, and you sometimes have trouble forgiving yourself, then please keep reading.

Isn't it curious that many of us are harder on ourselves than we are on others? We are more willing to accept God's forgiveness for others than we are his forgiveness for ourselves.

What I've come to see is that this isn't some kind of admirable humility or reverence for holiness. It's actually stacking one sin on top of another! And the second sin may be worse than the first. That's because, when we refuse to acknowledge God's forgiveness of ourselves, we are in effect saying that *we* are God—we get to decide what is forgiven and what is not forgiven.

Don't believe me?

Consider God's Word on this matter: "If we confess our sins, he is faithful and just and will forgive us our sins and purify us from all unrighteousness."[11] In light of that promise from God, if we think we are not forgiven even after we have repented, then we are actually getting up in God's face and saying, "Hey, God, *I* will decide who gets forgiven. *I* will decide who gets your unconditional love. Not *you*!"

Of course we should never take God's forgiveness for granted or treat it lightly. It's amazing grace! We should be forever grateful for receiving the acceptance from him that we do not deserve.

But for heaven's sake, let's not throw God's forgiveness back in his face. It's like receiving an extravagant birthday gift that overwhelms us with the generosity of the giver. It would be an incredible faux pas to say, "No. It's too much. Take it back." Instead, we have to receive the remarkable gift with all the humble gratitude we can muster.

When God forgives you, you need to agree with him. How exactly can you do this?

Perhaps all you need to do is say out loud, "I forgive myself for _____."
If you hear it with your ears, you'll be more likely to remember it and believe it.

Or perhaps you could think of some kind of ritual that will help you put your self-guilting behind you. When the Hebrews crossed the Jordan River into Canaan for the first time, God instructed them to build a monument out of river stones. This would remind future generations of this momentous occasion.[12] Is there some object you could use, or some action you could take, to ritualistically mark the momentous occasion of putting your guilt behind you?

Whatever it takes, your forgiveness of yourself should echo God's forgiveness of you.

Question 2: Do you regret hurting someone else?

Sometimes what we regret didn't involve other people; we only hurt ourselves. But in a world filled with social webs large and small, more often others have become casualties of our regrettable action, inaction, or reaction. We may have hurt others a lot or only a little, but either way, it's something we had better deal with if we want to move on.

Jason came home from work one day and said to his wife, Rebekah, "Guess what? Next Wednesday after work the boss is taking me and a couple of others from the office and our spouses out to dinner. He wants to honor us because of the way our team has turned the company around. You'll come, won't you?"[13]

Rebekah enthusiastically said she would be there. In fact, she was *so* enthusiastic that for just a moment Jason thought it was odd.

When Wednesday came around, Rebekah showed up, dressed to the nines, at the restaurant where Jason had asked her to meet him. She greeted him with a big smile. But then her smile faded as he ushered her to the back room where the other members of his office staff were seated. All through the event, Jason wondered why her posture was stiff and her smile seemed forced.

When they got home, he found out the reason.

This day was their wedding anniversary! When Jason had invited his wife to the business dinner, Rebekah had thought he was planning to surprise her with a special evening to celebrate their anniversary. She'd been sadly disappointed to learn that Jason had forgotten their anniversary and she would be forced to spend the evening with his coworkers.

Jason was horrified at what he had done. He apologized over and over. But when Rebekah left him in the guest room to sleep alone on their anniversary night, he knew he had hurt her so badly that it was going to take awhile to make up for this thoughtless move.

Here was a regret of inaction that was not sinful. But it *was* hurtful—very hurtful—to Rebekah.

In a situation like this, where you have hurt another, you have to do your best to bring healing to the wound you've inflicted. If possible, apologize to the person and ask forgiveness. Furthermore, if possible, make amends to the person for your wrongdoing and seek reconciliation. I repeat *if possible* because sometimes the other person isn't available, isn't willing, or isn't still alive to make things up with.

There may also be times when the person you've hurt or offended is available to make things up with, but when you give it a try, he or she refuses to grant forgiveness. This person is still holding the offense against you, as Rebekah held on to her grudge against Jason. At that point you can know that you've done everything you can, so resolve to let it go anyway. Stop dwelling on it in your mind. Forgive yourself. And meanwhile, keep hoping that reconciliation with the other person will be possible later.

The apostle Paul offers encouraging words emphasizing that we can be responsible only for our part in reconciliation. How the offended person responds is up to him or her. Paul says, "If it is possible, *as far as it depends on you,* live at peace with everyone."[14]

Question 3: Do you regret a mistake you made?

My brother, Jon, and his wife, Lisa, were taking a long-anticipated trip through Italy. They began in Venice, moved on to Florence, and then stopped in Rome. They had been sightseeing energetically for several days and were tired. So they decided to sleep in on their second day in Italy's capital and take it easy for the rest of the day.

At about 7:00 a.m. they were awakened when Jon's iPhone began to vibrate. Their eighteen-year-old son, Graham, wanted to FaceTime from back home.

Sleepily, and none too pleased about being woken up, Jon accepted the FaceTime request.

In the video call, Graham appeared to be standing on a city street at night. The first words out of his mouth were, "Dad, everyone is okay, but I just totaled the car."

Suddenly, Jon was wide awake.

As Graham continued his explanation, Jon learned that his son had been in Chicago with friends late in the evening, driving the family car. At the corner of Washington and LaSalle streets, a careless driver had struck them broadside. The police had already come and gone, and now a tow truck driver was winching up the wreckage.

Jon's anxiety level went down quickly when he realized that Graham and his friends really were unhurt. This initial call from Graham was followed by numerous texts and additional calls to the parents of the other kids who were in the car. Consequently, it was well into the early hours of the next morning before Jon or Lisa got another wink of sleep. So much for a relaxing day in Rome.

Like the good-hearted young man he is, my nephew kept apologizing for the incident. In turn, Jon kept reassuring him that an accident can happen to anybody and he was just glad nobody had been hurt.

Since then, whenever a recollection of the incident comes up, Jon grins and says, "It was just an accident"—here he pauses for dramatic effect—"that ended up costing us thousands of dollars."

Sometimes we have made a tactical blunder or committed an error in judgment, or have just taken a gamble and seen the dice roll against us, but it isn't a sin. It was an honest mistake or accident. There was no malicious intent, no moral failure involved. So we don't need to ask God's forgiveness for it. We only need to let ourselves off the hook.

What I want to say first is, don't be so hard on yourself. What you should have done always seems clearer in retrospect than it was at the time. This is called *hindsight bias*. Everybody's human. We all make mistakes. And those mistakes aren't always as bad as they seem when we're looking back. So don't keep kicking yourself.

Even if your mistake was serious and avoidable, remind yourself that it is something to learn from, not something to torment yourself over. An opportunity for positive feedback, remember? Forgive yourself. Let it go, my friend, let it go.

Question 4: Do you regret being hurt by someone else?

Ethicist Lewis Smedes has written that when you forgive, "You set a prisoner free, but you discover that the real prisoner was yourself."[15] So remember that forgiveness is like a Get Out of Jail Free card to set yourself free. Use it whenever anyone has hurt you.

If you read the book *Unbroken* or watched the movie based on it, you are familiar with Louis Zamperini, the former Olympic track athlete who spent two horrific years in Japanese prisoner-of-war camps during World War II. In particular, Zamperini was tormented by prison guard Mutsuhiro "Bird" Watanabe in ways that are difficult and painful to watch in the movie. For years after being released from prison, Zamperini dreamed of getting revenge on Bird and other Japanese soldiers who had mistreated him.

But then in 1949 he chose to follow Jesus at a Billy Graham crusade. The following year he traveled to Japan to visit Sugamo Prison, where many Japanese war criminals (not including Bird) were imprisoned. He embraced former guards he'd known and assured them he'd forgiven them. Years later, he tried to reach out to Bird to express his forgiveness to this man as well. Bird refused the meeting. But as far as Zamperini's well-being was concerned, it didn't matter. Forgiveness within his heart had long since set him free from the prison of hate.

You may be dealing with a reaction regret caused by something harmful that someone else did to you, perhaps lying to you, stealing from you, betraying you, neglecting you, or belittling you. Because the other person treated you like this, you got angry or bitter or vengeful toward him. Or maybe the poison traveled inward and you unreasonably started hating yourself for being the kind of person whom this could happen to. Whatever your toxic reaction might be, you know you cannot move on in life until you let go of it.

If somebody else has done something wrong to you, the answer is easy—forgive her. Easy to say, that is. Often hard to do. Yet you need to move in that direction, not just to release the other person but for yourself—to avoid the self-harm that holding a grudge can bring.

Now, I don't take forgiveness lightly. Sometimes the deeds that have been done to us were unbelievably cruel and hurtful, as was the case with Zamperini. That makes forgiving the wrongdoer terribly hard. The very idea of it might be repugnant to us. And honestly it might take awhile before we get to a point where we're genuinely able to forgive.

But Jesus forgave his murderers even as he hung dying on the cross.[16] More than that, God forgave *us* at the cross while *we* were still at odds with him.[17] His grace as the Great Forgiver is our model and power for forgiveness.[18] Thus the bottom line: "Forgive one another if any of you has a grievance against someone. Forgive as the Lord forgave you."[19]

We can always learn how to be better forgivers. Recently, I got schooled about forgiveness in a way I will not soon forget.

MERCY ON HIS SOUL

In June 2015, I had a day off, and I was getting some chores done around the house. While I sat at my kitchen table paying some bills, I was streaming the news on my iPhone when they cut to a live report. The bond hearing was under way for Dylann Roof, a young man who two days before had shot nine people at Emanuel AME Church in Charleston, South Carolina.

I stopped everything I was doing to watch. I was both shocked and inspired as one victim's family member after another had an opportunity to make a statement to Roof, but instead of condemning, they offered him forgiveness.

These are some highlights.[20]

- *The daughter of victim Ethel Lance:* "I forgive you. You took something very precious away from me. I will never get to talk to her ever again. I will never be able to hold her again, but I forgive you, and have mercy on your soul."

- *A relative of Myra Thompson:* "I forgive him and my family forgives him. But we would like him to take this opportunity to repent. Repent. Confess. Give your life to the one who matters most: Christ."

- *The sister of DePayne Middleton Doctor:* "For me, I'm a work in progress. And I acknowledge that I am very angry. But one thing that DePayne always enjoined in our family . . . is she taught me that we are the family that love built. We have no room for hating, so we have to forgive. I pray God on your soul."

Journalists covering the story were speechless at these words. I found them astounding to listen to as well.

Do you know what I think we were witnessing during that bond hearing? Through those precious Christ followers in Charleston, we got a glimpse of people experiencing God's release through forgiveness. The hurt they felt was immense, but they would not get stuck. They were starting over.

Question 5: Do you regret the pain you feel from life circumstances?

With this last question, we're moving beyond the realm of human sin and recklessness to the vast area made up of regrets that are impersonal in their origin . . . and therefore can be even harder to deal with.

Here's the picture:

You develop a chronic illness. A hurricane sweeps away your home. The stock market turns south, and you're once again doubting your financial future. Sometimes there is no one to blame, really, neither yourself nor anybody else, for the regret you feel. It's merely life's circumstances that have caused your regret. Every day, regrettable things happen even when no one has intended it.

Not long ago, the Chicago area was hit by what is often referred to as a hundred-year flood. My family came through it unscathed, but one day we got a call from our friends Dan and Shannon, who said they had water in their basement and were asking for help. My wife, Sue, and I left the kids with their grandparents and drove to the older part of town where Dan and Shannon lived. After taking many detours around flooded areas, we finally got there.

Dan took us to the interior door leading to his basement. That's when I realized the true extent of the disaster. We weren't talking about a few inches of water on the basement floor. The level of the water was to the top of the basement stairway, just one step below the door!

Down in the basement, our friends kept not only cleaning supplies, holiday decorations, and other easily replaceable stuff but also most of their family's priceless memorabilia. Photo albums. Artwork from when the kids were little. Awards. Crafts. Shannon's wedding dress. Inherited keepsakes. All underwater and all ruined.

Shannon cried. Dan looked grim. In just one night, without anyone really to blame, they experienced a loss they had never anticipated.

Along with some other friends, Sue and I helped this couple get their lives back together once the floodwaters finally receded. They would regret this disaster for a long time to come. It was as if nature had reached out its watery fingers and snatched something precious from them.

As we said when considering the Fall in chapter 1, the world we live in is often hard and seemingly hostile. And so, even though we don't have a personal subject to blame, we can feel anger and resentment toward our circumstances. In a sense, we have to forgive the fallen world for the disease or disaster or other impersonal circumstance that has been hurtful toward us. And we have to guard against having an emotional reaction to this regret that will make the situation worse.

I offer a special caution about this kind of situation: when the world has hurt you, resist the temptation to blame God. He's never the author of evil. He made the world good and, at the cost of his own Son, is in the process of restoring it to goodness. He grieves right alongside you, and he wants you to share with him how you are feeling about the harm you're suffering. So don't curse or blame God. "Forgive" him—that is, quit placing false blame on him. Don't run from him but rather run toward him for comfort and guidance. He will give you what you need to release you from the pain you feel.

EXERCISE YOUR "RELEASE" MUSCLES

Last January it occurred to me that over the previous six weeks of holiday celebrations I had eaten way too much turkey, Chex Party Mix, and cheese coffee cake and had not been out running nearly enough. So, I did what a lot of people do at New Year's: I made a resolution and joined the local YMCA.

But I've discovered something since then. Just signing a contract and making monthly payments to the Y has done nothing for my physical condition. I still don't have six-pack abs or buns of steel. Sure, I decided to join. But what I'm realizing is that I actually have to *go* to the gym to get in shape. What a revelation!

It's the same with releasing our regrets. It's so easy to put off this step. Even after you've evaluated what you need to do and used the five starting-over questions, you could still set this book down and go on with life as usual.

Don't make that mistake!

Start practicing release as soon as possible. Ask for forgiveness. Extend forgiveness to others. Forgive yourself.

I'm going to give you some tips that might help you get into motion.

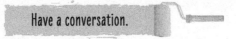

Have a conversation.

Whether you've hurt others through a sin or a mistake, or others have hurt you in some way, you will likely need to have a conversation to try to get some resolution in the relationship. Maybe you need to make a phone call or ask another person for a meeting to talk it out.

By asking for forgiveness or granting forgiveness, you will begin to experience the release of regret. The person on the other end of the conversation may be ready and willing to hear your request for forgiveness or to respond to you by saying, "I'm sorry." You'll never know until you have the conversation.

Do it soon. Today's good, right?

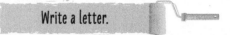

Write a letter.

Or maybe a conversation won't work. Maybe the other person involved in your regret won't talk to you. Maybe you're worried that you won't be able to manage your words properly in a conversation. Or maybe, given what's gone on, a face-to-face would just be too awkward for both sides.

In that case you've got another option: write a letter or an e-mail. I know it seems old school, but a written letter feels more thoughtful and can't be electronically forwarded. Do not send a text—that would be too brief and impersonal. In a letter, write about your point of view and what you think needs to happen next. Be careful as you compose this note, because you want to make matters better and not worse, but be honest and forthright.

If putting the words down is hard, remember that you're writing this letter not just for the other person but also for yourself. So that you can experience release.

One advantage of letter writing is that you can do it even if the addressee couldn't read it if you sent it, such as when a formerly abusive parent is now lost in dementia or has died. It will still be restorative for you to put your thoughts and feelings down in written words.

Pray.

There's yet another option available, regardless of your circumstances.

Talk to God about the regret you've kept bottled up. Offer a prayer asking God for supernatural power to forgive and to put the past behind. The Bible says we should pray for our enemies, so pray also for the good of those who have hurt you.[21] Wrestle with God in prayer, if that's what you need to do, and then wait in an attitude of surrender to receive his blessing of peace. As you release your regret, God will release you from it.

I think back to my own prayer in that quiet room at my second college. I was agonizing before God about the confusing and painful events that had forced me to leave my previous school. It was all a big mess. I didn't understand what it meant or what good could come from it.

But at least, in my naiveté, I did what I needed to do with my messy regrets. I took them to God. I began to release them to him.

And in turn, he released me from them.

In retrospect, what's truly amazing to me is that God responded to my prayers of release by beginning to reorient my future in ways I never could have anticipated—and he did it immediately! You see, after that prayer, I got up off my knees and went to my first class at a brand-new school. It was in that very first class that I met a friend who would change my life and lead me back to Chicago to start a church.

I didn't know it then, but beginning with that prayer, God was redeeming my regret.

In the next chapter I'm going to show you how you too can see God redeem your regrets. It's not out of reach. In fact, it's closer than you think.

CHAPTER 5

STEP #3: REDEEM YOUR REGRETS

A nineteenth-century English teenager named William Webb Ellis loved playing cricket and football (that's soccer to us Americans) at his school. He was a passionate competitor in school sports, although reputed to be "rather inclined to take unfair advantage at football."[1]

According to reports published later, Webb Ellis was playing in a football game at his school in 1823 when his inclination to take unfair advantage got the better of him. In a game where players were not supposed to handle the ball, Ellis *picked up the ball* and ran with it toward the goal.

No one today knows what the reaction on the field was to Ellis's transgression. Most likely, he got called back by an official. It's easy to imagine the spectators and the other players jeering at him. Ellis probably regretted his violation of the rules of football.

Nevertheless, apparently his actions were not soon forgotten. Someone seems to have said, "Hey, why *not* let the players carry the ball?" In any case, by the 1840s, the game of football as played at his school had evolved to a point where it was ruled acceptable to handle the ball.

The name of that school?

Rugby.

Yes, William Webb Ellis was the unwitting originator of rugby football and today is still honored by having the cup for the world championship of this sport called the William Webb Ellis Cup. If you go to Rugby School in England today, you'll see a statue representing Webb Ellis as a schoolboy athlete running with a football in his hands.

Not many of us in the United States are particularly familiar with rugby football. But a great many of us (including a couple of authors named Ferguson) are fans of another sport that eventually developed out of that one—American football.

Quite possibly, there would be no "Friday night lights" at high school stadiums across the country, no college bowl games with painted fanatics in the stands, no three-hundred-pound NFL players with their multimillion-dollar contracts if it hadn't been for a rule violation committed by an overeager schoolboy nearly two centuries ago.

Some unexpected and remarkable things came out of a situation that for a while looked like a big mistake.

That's redemption.

THE REDEMPTION OF YOUR CIRCUMSTANCES

To exit the Sorry Cycle and start over, first we must recognize our regret and then we release it. The third and final step in the process is best described by the term *redeem*. No other word so richly defines the way we break free from regret and move ahead.

Redemption will urge you to take the long view. How you perceive your regret right now isn't how you will see it in the future. Trust God to make something good out of it.

The Greek word for redemption is *lytrōsis,* and it literally means "a ransoming, deliverance" or "a rescue." In the New Testament, it is used preeminently to describe what Jesus did by giving up his life for us more than two thousand years ago on the cross. But it also reminds us that Jesus delivers us from our regrets and can make something beautiful out of them.

Historically, the word for "redemption" was used in reference to the purchase of a slave's freedom. A slave was "redeemed" when the price was paid for his freedom. Why is that relevant? Because we can choose to be enslaved by our regrets, or we can let God redeem our regrets and find a freedom only he can give through Jesus.

When God goes to work on our area of regret, he sets us free from our captivity to the Sorry Cycle. He takes what we once considered a loss and turns it into a gain. He restores the hope we had thought was gone forever.

What sets this part of the process apart from the previous two steps (recognize and release) is that redemption is *not something we do*. Rather, it is *something only God can do*. What we have to do is willingly bring our regrets to him and ask him to do with our regrets what only he can do—make something beautiful out of them.

I can't tell you in advance what your redemption is going to look like. But whatever your redemption turns out to be, I know it will be something incredible. A mistake turned into a miracle. Evil converted to good. Tragedy transformed into opportunity.

In the same chapter where he talks about all people and nature longing for God, the apostle Paul says, "In all things God works for the good of those who love him, who have been called according to his purpose."[2] *All* things. Even our regrets.

God's redemption doesn't erase whatever it was that happened to cause us regret. But his redemption does set it in a larger context of goodness, transforming the darkness of the past into the brightness of a new future.

Let me give you another way of looking at it . . .

REDEEMED AND RECYCLED

When I was a kid, soft drinks (or pop, as we call it in Chicago) were sold in glass bottles. To me, there was nothing quite as refreshing as an ice-cold Coca-Cola in a glass bottle.

And there was an added bonus that came with that glass bottle. When I finished drinking from it, I would take that seemingly useless bottle down to the

White Hen Pantry, where the owner, Marv, would redeem it for a dime. That was almost enough to buy a pack of baseball cards.

I redeemed that old bottle for a pack of baseball cards!

That still wasn't the end. Because do you know what the Coca-Cola Company was going to do with that bottle? They were going to recycle it.

Well, God is in the same business—redeeming and recycling. He's always been into taking the worst, the least, or the last in people's lives and turning it into something so much more.

- Jacob was a thief and a con man. God redeemed and recycled his conniving, and he became the father of a nation.
- Moses was a murderer, but God redeemed and recycled his rage and hatred, and he became the greatest leader in Israel's history.
- Ruth was an idol worshiper. But God redeemed and recycled her paganism, and she became an ancestor of Jesus Christ.
- David was an adulterer, a murderer. God redeemed and recycled his passion, and he became the greatest of the kings.
- Esther was a harem girl. God redeemed and recycled her sex appeal, and she saved the Jewish people from history's first holocaust.
- Peter was boastful, impulsive, and an inconsistent man who cussed like a sailor. God redeemed and recycled his pride and flaws, and Peter became a fearless apostolic leader in the early church.
- Mary Magdalene was a prostitute. God redeemed and recycled her immorality, and she became a saint.
- Zacchaeus was a greedy, cheating, dishonest man. God redeemed and recycled his miserliness and underhanded business practices, and he became a disciple of Jesus.
- Paul was a persecutor of the early Christian movement. God redeemed and recycled his closed-minded legalism and turned him into the greatest missionary in history.

What about you? What is the worst in you? What is least in you? What are the dregs of your life? What are the worst parts of your past? Got any trash buried anywhere? God wants to redeem it, to recycle it, to turn tragedy and awfulness and shame into a source of healing and wholeness for you and for others.[3]

When God does that, you know what that is? That's redemption.

THE FACES OF REDEMPTION

My redemption is different from your redemption is different from somebody else's redemption. Each time God redeems someone's difficult situation, it is perfectly adapted for him or her. Isn't it amazing to think of the creative ways God is working in complex, difficult situations all over the world all the time to bring about good? Now that's a God I can gladly follow!

Your redemption might look something like one of these categories:

Redemption can look like finding your way back to God.

Many people, after taking treacherous detours in life, find themselves considering questions of spiritual depth and ultimate meaning as never before. They often take a second look at God. And when they do, they find him waiting for them with open arms, like the father in Jesus's parable welcoming the lost son home.[4]

Redemption can look like spiritual growth.

Seeing the bottom fall out of your self-made plans can drop you to your knees in humility—the perfect posture for seeing the true magnitude of God's greatness. Recognizing the harm your sin has done can renew your commitment to pursuing holiness. Getting stuck in a waiting period can encourage you to pick up the spiritual disciplines, such as prayer and fasting. Watching God start to act in redemption can inspire outbursts of praise and worship. A pattern of starting over in life through God's grace builds up an impenetrable trust in him.

Redemption can look like rescheduling.

Perhaps your first business start-up failed, but later you might be ready to make a success of another entrepreneurial attempt. Maybe you and your spouse wanted children as soon as you married, but the first child didn't come until years later. In situations like this, if God delays giving you a gift, it's because he knows the right time for you to receive it better than you do.

The most mature Jesus followers I know have developed a reflex reaction to timing surprises: they simply accept God's scheduling, trusting that he knows best. Because he does.

Redemption can look like redirection.

I can look back at so many times in my life when I was upset because I didn't get what I wanted—and now I'm so thankful I didn't! In retrospect, I realize that I would have been sorry if I had gotten the outcome I wanted. Or that, if I had gotten it, I would have missed out on something better later on.

Can you relate?

I think of a young woman I know who was distraught nearly to the point of suicide when her fiancé broke their engagement. But in time, she met and married another man—and she knows he's so much better for her than the other guy could ever have been.

Then there's the business exec whose story I've followed for years. He wanted to become a pastor, but for several reasons it didn't work out. Yet today he's a C-suite powerhouse executive making a remarkable difference in the lives of many people in his industry. He's glad now that he didn't become a pastor, because he now knows that God has him exactly where he is supposed to be.

I wouldn't be surprised if God sometimes looks down on us from heaven and chuckles as he says, "Take it easy. I've got something awesome in store for you that you could never guess."

Redemption can look like blessing.

Job in the Old Testament lost everything he had, except his life, through a series of calamities. For a long time he was stuck in a Sorry Cycle, going over and over his losses in his mind, fruitlessly trying to figure them out. Then God presented him with the stark fact of his own sovereignty and right to do as he wished. So

Job at last released his regrets, laying them before God. And then God redeemed Job's regret in spectacular fashion by giving him a new wife, more children, and more wealth than he'd had in the beginning.

That's another model of redemption. We outlast a period of barrenness and lack, only to see God in his own good time pour abundance into our lap.

Redemption can look like a chance to bless others.

I know recovering drug addicts who have become drug counselors, helping others along their journey of healing. I know former teenage rebels who are teaching today's youth how to avoid costly mistakes. Their regrets have been turned inside out by redemption, and others are the beneficiaries. In fact, I would go so far as to say that people who haven't suffered much don't have much to teach others.

Redemption often takes the form of a gift of service to others; it's as if God says, *"Help others with what you have learned in your hard times."* And we know that when we bless others, we are blessed in return. Redemption is always rewarding.

On the other side of your regret, what kind of redemption might be staring back at you?

THE UNLIMITED PROMISE OF REDEMPTION

God's power of redemption is comprehensive and unlimited. He can bring redemption no matter what type of regret you're dealing with.

Are there missteps you've made that cause you to groan or make your face burn with embarrassment when you think about them? God can redeem your regrets of *action*.

Do you grieve the missed opportunities of the past; things you should have done but didn't? God has redemption for your regrets of *inaction*.

Perhaps you have responded poorly to tragic circumstances, reacting with shame, blame, or bitterness. God will redeem your regrets of *reaction* too.

I've seen God bring about redemption in my life in all three of these kinds of regrets, and I've seen him do the same in the lives of many others.

Life After Porn: Redemption for a Regret of Action

Crissy Moran was just the sort of woman that the porn industry so often pulls into its greedy grasp. Very attractive. And emotionally broken.[5]

The roots of her dysfunction ran deep, with both Crissy and the people closest to her making choices that she would come to regret. Her father was an alcoholic, and her parents divorced when she was a preteen. Crissy lived with her mom, but their relationship was frequently contentious. Then at the age of seventeen she found herself pregnant. Her boyfriend reneged on his promise to marry her, and her mom took her to get an abortion. Crissy sank into depression.

From this point, she became a self-described relationship addict, going from boyfriend to boyfriend. When these serial relationships didn't satisfy her need to feel loved, she started doing porn, hoping the adulation of her fans would fill the empty space in her heart. After six years in that industry, the inherent destructiveness of selling her body, combined with abandonment by another boyfriend she had hoped to marry, brought her to the point of wanting to take her own life.

"I didn't think I could deal with any more heartache," Crissy recalled, "and that is when I cried out to God and begged him to show me he was real. Two days later he sent someone into my life to talk to me about his love for me. No one had mentioned God to me since I was a little girl. I knew this wasn't a coincidence and that God was really pursuing me."[6]

She placed her trust in Jesus that very day and began a deep healing process, which included sexual abstinence and two years without even going on a date. Eventually she married a youth minister and joined him in his work.

"God is able to redeem, restore and heal," Crissy testified. "He has done so in many areas in my life." He has restored her relationship with her mother, given her friends to help overcome her lifelong loneliness, brought healing to her depression and anxiety, and given her a godly man who loves her.

The List of His Wrongs: Redemption for a Regret of Inaction

Several years ago, a married couple—Ted and Sue—asked if I would talk with them about some struggles in their marriage.[7] I was shocked when they informed me they were on the brink of divorce. They had been a part of our church for years, and from the outside, they looked like they had it all together.

At first, their gripes with each other seemed pretty normal to me and not unduly concerning. But then Sue reached in her purse and pulled out a piece of notebook paper.

"What's that?" I asked.

"This is where I've written down all the ways Ted has hurt me," Sue said. And she began to read from the lengthy list.

As she did so, 1 Corinthians 13:5 flashed into my mind—a verse that says true love "keeps no record of wrongs." Yet that was literally what Sue had done— kept a record of Ted's wrongs!

I glanced at Ted. The color was draining from his face.

"Wait, wait!" I interrupted Sue's recitation of errors. "You're telling me that you've been keeping a list of everything Ted has done wrong? Have you *talked* with Ted about these things?"

"Well . . . some of them," Sue said hesitantly.

We went on to discuss how it can make matters worse to hold on to grievances rather than go to the other person right away and try to deal with them constructively. Sue began to see that failing to confront Ted hadn't been such a good idea. She had a dawning regret of inaction.

That little insight sparked a new beginning in their marriage. In time, Ted and Sue both agreed to release one another from the past through forgiveness. Of course it took work and time, but it took their marriage to a far better place.

They went on to share their story at marriage conferences, discouraging other couples from making a similar mistake of bottling up resentment instead of getting it out in the open. Sue will pull out the notebook paper with Ted's wrongs on it and wave it in front of the crowd as an illustration of what not to do.

Chelsea's Light: Redemption for a Regret of Reaction

On a mild February afternoon, seventeen-year-old Chelsea King set out for a run in a San Diego community park. She never came back.

Her parents, Brent and Kelly King, became concerned and called the police. Law enforcement officers and thousands of volunteers searched the area for days. Eventually the Kings' worst fears were realized. Someone found Chelsea's body in a shallow grave beside Lake Hodges. She'd been raped and murdered. A convicted sex offender eventually pleaded guilty and went to jail for the crime.

What's amazing is how God has brought a light for others out of that dark experience.

Within months of their daughter's death, Brent and Kelly established a nonprofit called Chelsea's Light Foundation to bring communities together around protecting children. Most notably, the King family and their foundation were successful in promoting Chelsea's Law. The California legislature unanimously passed the law increasing penalties, parole provisions, and oversight for sex offenders who attack children. More than nine million kids in the state are safer today because of this law.

Their son, Tyler, later wrote and produced a documentary film called *Chelsea's Light: A Brother's Journey* about what it's like to grieve and recover from the loss of a loved one to a sexual predator.

Brent, Kelly, and Tyler now live in the Chicago area and over the last few years have become my good friends and a part of the church I lead. So I have been privileged to observe firsthand how they have dealt with the aftermath of this terrible loss.

When Chelsea was brutally stolen from them, the Kings could have gotten lost in anger, withdrawal, substance misuse, or any number of other counterproductive reactions to the tragedy they regretted. And I know they were tempted by some of them. But instead, God has used them to bring great good out of the most horrific of situations.

Waiting on the Edge of Your Seat

Redemption is the work of God.

If we tried, you or I might be able to correct some errors of the past and engineer a better outcome than we've had so far. But if we're looking for a truly *supernatural* change in our circumstances, one that we're not capable of producing and probably couldn't even imagine ahead of time, then we have to look to God for it. Our part is to trust him.

This trust isn't a dull sort of idleness; we don't just sit around hoping something will happen. Nor is it a self-generated "hope against hope" that depends on our working up our emotions inside ourselves. Instead, it's an eager expectation and a peaceful confidence that God will act in his own way in his own time. It's based on what we know of God's character and how he has consistently acted in the past.

This kind of trust is also an active trust. As we're waiting for God to bring about redemption, we need to continue to maintain our relationship with God, just as Paul and Silas prayed and sang praises to God in their prison cell *before* an earthquake delivered them to freedom.[8] It's also important that we keep on obeying God, because if we expect him to be faithful to us, we must be faithful to him. And we should take whatever preparatory steps we think God might choose to use to bring about our redemption in time.

If you're hoping for God to send you a spouse, maybe you need to put yourself in places where you'll meet single people.

If you are craving a more challenging career, perhaps it's time to go back to school.

If you want a restored relationship with somebody you're estranged from, maybe you could start talking with him or her.

Although you can't engineer your own redemption, you can partner with God in it. The preparation may put you in a better place to receive his grace, and in the meantime it will sustain your eager expectation for what he wants to do.

Then when the redemption does come, you will be able to receive it as a gift from the God who loves you. The more you experience his redemption of your regrets, the easier it will be to trust him and go along with whatever he wills.

If trusting God for redemption seems scary or risky to you, think about this comparison:

Do you remember what it was like when you walked out on a diving board for the first time, preparing to jump into the deep end? If you were like me, you were more than a little doubtful about whether that was such a good idea. You couldn't imagine anything good coming out of what you were about to do. But after you went ahead with it, you realized that you had not only survived the jump but had actually enjoyed it.

It's the same way with trusting God for redemption. It can seem hard to do, but once we've tried it and have not only survived it but are also enjoying the cool waters of redemption, we are much more willing to get back on the diving board and trust him with our regrets again.

As trust becomes a habit, we'll begin to more accurately recognize God's ways of working out his will in our lives. We'll understand that his redemption is intended to not only bless us but more importantly to bring honor and glory to him. Praise will become the dominant note in the symphony of our lives.

Redemption can become a way of life. For "God . . . acts on behalf of those who wait for him."[9]

WISH FULFILLMENT

In the next five chapters, I'm going to be applying the three Rs—recognize, release, redeem—to some of the biggest areas of regret people have. Do any of these wistful regrets resonate with you?

- "I wish I had thought about God more."
- "I wish I had loved and been loved better."
- "I wish I had taken better care of myself."

- "I wish I had been smarter about money."
- "I wish I had given my life to a big cause."

Spirituality. Relationships. Health. Finances. Purpose. When people are surveyed about ways in which they wish they could start over, these areas of life are consistently among their greatest regrets. If I were to venture a guess, I would say that you have regrets either large or small in all five of these areas and that at least one "I wish . . ." statement reminds you of a deep pain in your heart right now.

Peace to you, my friend. You don't have to be bound by regrets in any of these areas any longer.

Redemption awaits.

REDEEMING YOUR DEEPEST REGRETS

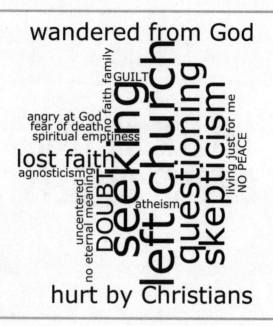

wandered from God

GUILT
angry at God
fear of death
spiritual emptiness
lost faith
agnosticism
uncentered
no eternal meaning
DOUBT
seeking
left church
no faith family
questioning
skepticism
atheism
living just for me
NO PEACE

hurt by Christians

CHAPTER 6

FINDING YOUR WAY BACK

SPIRITUALITY REGRET: "I wish I had thought about God more."

My wife, Sue, and I sat down at Standard Market, one of our favorite lunch spots near our home, for a Friday afternoon date. We had just started eating and talking when a young lady left her nearby table and hustled over to ours. She put her hands on our table, leaned in, and said, "I'm sorry for bothering you, but can I just tell you something?"

I knew the answer had to be "Yes."

She began to explain. "Eight weeks ago, my husband and I had separated and we were both feeling hopeless about the future of our family. We were having conversations about what to do with the kids and how we would be better parents separate than we were together. But then about a month ago both my husband and I got invited independently to your church without either of us knowing the other got invited. We both came on the same Sunday without the knowledge that we were both there, and it was the Sunday you started the *Finding Your Way Back to God* series. We both came for all five weeks of the series. We both started reading your book, we agreed to go to counseling together, and now we have moved back in together."

She paused to breathe. The tears started to flow. As I jumped up to give her a hug, she wiped away the tears and said, "I think we are going to make it! And I just wanted to say, 'Thank you.'"

Her marriage had been stuck in the Sorry Cycle. Both she and her husband had been longing for something better. Both had made choices they regretted. And it looked like the regret was going to win. But then all that changed when they found their way back to God.

In the next weeks and months, I got to know this energetic young woman, Aimee, and her husband, Joe. Every week they would sit in the row right behind me at church and would regularly express gratitude for finding God. When I asked them about using their story in this book on regrets, they gave me their permission and then Aimee said, "Tell 'em, don't wait so long to pursue a relationship with God!"

So consider yourself told.

I meet people every day who are in the same place as Aimee and Joe were, struggling on their journey back to God. The particular circumstances are different, but they have the same kind of spiritual yearning within. Some of them have never had anything to do with God or spiritual matters before, but now they wonder if they have missed out on something important. Some of them once believed in God but for one reason or another drifted away from a life of faith. Some of them, like Aimee and Joe, have been trying to make some part of their life work but realize they can't do it on their own—they need a source of help greater than themselves.

These people will often look back on an earlier period of their lives and reflect, *I wish I had thought about God more.* They might be hung up on that regret, feeling discouraged that so much of life has been wasted or passed them by. But I *love* to hear people say that, because I know they are primed to start over!

Regardless of who you are, what sort of faith background you have, and where you are in life, you can begin a journey toward God today. It's a journey you can embark upon in confidence. As Jon and I reminded people in our book *Finding Your Way Back to God,* the Lord says, "You will seek me and find me when you seek me with all your heart. I will be found by you."[1] Even more than you want to be reunited with God, he wants to be reunited with you.

OUT OF A DISTANT COUNTRY

Jesus told a story that starts with a young man who is tired of waiting for his father to die so that he can live the way he wants.[2] The young man makes a demand: "Dad, I want my share of your estate. Now."

A son in Jesus's day was not only expected to wait until his father died before he would receive his inheritance, but he was also expected to take care of his father in his old age. So this is a huge offense. The father is crushed. Nevertheless, he gives his son the money and watches him disappear down the road as the son sets off for a distant country.

Now the son finally has the chance to live it up like he wants. He parties with prostitutes and generally lives life on the wild side. And it is fun.

At first.

But then it all takes a turn. The party lights go out, and all he has left in the morning is a room full of empties, a phone number written on the mirror with lipstick, and an awful emptiness inside. The life he wants turns out to be the life he hates.

Then he goes broke.

The young man gets so desperate that he hires himself out to feed pigs, then gets so hungry that the slop he is throwing to the pigs starts looking tasty. But he isn't even allowed to eat the pigs' food.

That's when he comes to his senses. He recognizes his regret. He wants to go back home and start over. But how can he? He has already taken his share of home and squandered every last dollar of it.

Finally he decides that if he can't go back home as a son, maybe he can go back as a servant. He knows that his dad's employees have more food than he does. Maybe if he offers to return home and join them in their work, his dad will accept him on that basis.

As the lost son heads for home, he doesn't know how his father will respond. He knows he has blown it big time, and he figures all-out rejection is a possibility. So he spends his time on the road rehearsing his prepared apology. He is ready to release his regret by asking his father's forgiveness.

What happens next stuns the young man.

As he approaches the old homestead, his father spots him at once—it's as if he had never stopped watching for his lost son. In a move totally unexpected for a respected head of household in his culture, the father comes running. He throws his arms around his son whom he thought was lost for good, and he refuses to let go. It is an embrace that neither will ever forget.

The son, who was prepared to clear whatever bar his father set, finds that there is no bar. No lectures. No standoffishness. No need for promises of doing better. No requirement to grovel or prove his sincerity. Just open arms and tears of joy and celebration. Redemption has already begun.

The symbolism in the parable of the lost son is pretty obvious.

- The younger son = anybody who is far from God.
- The father = God.
- Coming home = finding a relationship with God.

Are you a lost son or daughter? Do you want to find God? I assure you that he's reaching out to you, loving you despite everything you've done and everything you've been through. And when you find your way to your Father, he will greet you with the words, "Dear child of mine, welcome home!"

KEZAZAH

I told the story of the lost son in great detail in *Finding Your Way Back to God*. But there was one nuance of the story that I did not mention in my previous book. I want to tell it to you now because it illustrates a type of fear that keeps many of us in the Sorry Cycle when it comes to our spirituality. I'm talking about the fear of rejection.

Ask yourself, *Why was the son in the story so reluctant to come home for help?*

Yes, going home would mean admitting he'd made mistakes. It would be un-pleasant and feel shameful. Yet given that he was broke, lonely, and hungrier than a hog, wouldn't his need outweigh his pride just a little?

A little-known Jewish custom from Jesus's time period might help us under-stand his reluctance. It's called *kezazah* (pronounced kay-zah-zah), and it was used to disown community members who had, well, behaved badly in some way.

If a young Jewish man had abandoned his family, squandered his wealth disreputably among Gentiles, and now was coming home, hoping to start over where he had begun, members of the community would meet him at the city gate. A leader for the community would bring with him a clay pot. And in front of the returnee, this leader would ceremoniously throw the pot to the ground, where it would shatter into countless pieces.

Then the leader would pick up one of the shards, hold it where the young man could see it, and deliver a rebuke along these lines:

"This is the brokenness that you have caused in our community. You have broken trust. You have broken relationship. You have broken the heart of your father. The damage is beyond repair. So let this be a symbol of your own broken life.

"You are not whole. You are not family. You are not welcome.

"You are cut off!"

The word *kezazah* means "cutting off." With such treatment, the young man would know he was no longer welcome at home and had been cut off from his community forever. So he would have to turn around and head out into the world again, friendless and alone.

I wish I could say that this awful custom had no counterparts in today's world, but sadly, that's not true. There are times when religious communities try to squeeze people out who they don't think fit in or measure up. It's not always as obvious as saying, "Get out of our church. You don't belong here!" But then again, it's not necessary to be obvious. A little whispering, a little cold-shouldering can make it clear to a newcomer that he or she doesn't match the approved profile.

Maybe one reason you haven't made more progress in your journey in the heavenly Father's direction is that you fear the reaction of religious people if you tried to join them. How would people at a church react if they knew about your background? Or if they knew the questions and doubts you're still wrestling with?

Maybe you've had uncomfortable run-ins with religious people in the past, and that history is causing you to struggle with the idea of returning to God.

As much as it hurts me as a pastor to say this, it *is* possible that you might show up at a church and find the welcome mat withdrawn. I beg you not to let that possibility stop you. There are lots of other churches where people will accept you despite flaws in your behavior and despite the fact that you are still trying to figure out what you believe and where you belong.

Perhaps one reason the father in Jesus's story ran to the lost son was that he wanted to get to him first, before any members of the community could send the son back out into the cold. The same is true for you: it's the heavenly Father's welcome that matters, not any community's possible rejection of you.

Don't hesitate. Keep on seeking for God. You can find him as you recognize, release, and redeem your spirituality regret.

Recognize & Release Tool

To help you assess and deal with your own spirituality regrets (as well as all other types of regrets), use the tool in the back of this book, the Living Beyond Regrets Work Sheet.

SOME WHO WANDER ARE LOST

You may be saying, "I wish I had thought more about God" because you're going through a crisis that's causing you to reevaluate what you really need and what you really believe. Or maybe a sense of your distance from God has been slowly building in your consciousness to the point where you're finally determined to do something about it. Either way, it's time to recognize your regret.

Remember, don't regret your regret. You should love it, because it gives you feedback and can teach you how to start over.

Start by simply identifying your regret regarding spirituality. State it to yourself. Perhaps the three buckets will help.

- Do you have a regret of action when it comes to God? Examples: *I wish I hadn't quit going to church when I went to college. I wish I hadn't settled for just going through the motions of religion. I wish I hadn't gotten so defensive about my lifestyle that I turned away from God.*

- Do you have a spirituality regret of inaction? Examples: *I wish I had listened when my friend told me about her faith. I wish I had given church a try. I wish I had explored my questions about suffering and miracles instead of just quitting on God. I wish I had made the effort to read the Bible for myself.*

- Do you have a spirituality regret of reaction? Examples: *I wish I hadn't gotten so mad at hypocrites and mean-spirited Christians that I turned away from God. I wish I hadn't let the pain of my life embitter me toward God. I wish I hadn't gone along so compliantly with my skeptic friends.*

What are the facts in the case—the *who, what, when, where, why,* and *how*? Perhaps there have been stages in your journey away from God. Maybe there have been turning points or particular influences you should be aware of.

Next, label your emotions regarding the distance you feel from God. Perhaps you're angry. Or lonely. Or scared. Maybe a creative description will help—for example, "My distance from God feels as cold as the emptiness of space."

What does your regret regarding God tell you that you need to do more of, do less of, or do differently? For example, maybe you need to take time to explore Jesus and the Bible. Or quit making fun of Christians and start getting to know them as real people. Or stop letting morality issues keep you from the more essential issue of faith.

WIPING YOUR SOUL SLATE CLEAN

When we're distant from God, we often feel like we're living in a vacuum. But life doesn't happen in a vacuum. Over time, people and events have combined to keep us from God or even push us away from God. But if you want to experience God's fullest redemption, then you will want to make amends by seeking to forgive and be forgiven.

Think of these acts of forgiveness as loosing chains until you're entirely free of your regret. Think of them as sweeping away emotional and spiritual debris so that your life becomes a clean foundation for God to build his redemption upon. This process of letting go of your God regrets is too important to skip.

Ask forgiveness of others.

While some people may have driven you away from God, there may have been others who graciously and gently nurtured your faith—but you ignored them, blew them off, or worse. To experience the release and redemption you want, go to them and make things right, to the extent that you can, by apologizing.

Forgive others.

As you look back on your life, it may become clear that someone helped to lead you away from God. Maybe a church leader touched you inappropriately, and afterward you didn't want anything to do with church or God. Or maybe an atheistic professor in college tore apart your youthful belief system. Or maybe some friends mocked you until you stopped going to church.

No one could *force* you to stop giving thought to God, but they could *encourage* a lack of spiritual interest. Let me be clear: you have a legitimate grievance with what they did. But holding on to a grudge against them will only chain you to the Sorry Cycle. To the best of your ability, begin to forgive them for their part in putting distance between you and God.

Ask forgiveness of God.

Let me take a risk and introduce a word that has gotten a bad rap: *repentance*. We only seem to hear the word *repent* in connection with hellfire and brimstone. Seems as if repentance is most often used as a scare tactic. Let's get a fuller understanding of repentance by seeing how the Bible uses it.

- *Metanoia* is the Greek word for "repent," and we find it throughout the New Testament. It means "changing one's mind."
- *Teshuvah* is the Hebrew word for "repent" found in the Old Testament. It means "to return to where you belong."

So repentance means to *change your thinking* and to *return to the place where you belong*. Repentance is necessary if we want to find our way back to God. It means we change the direction of our lives and go back to the God who loves us; it means we ask him to forgive us for all the ways we have hurt him, others, and ourselves.

Finding your way back to God is all about the restoration of a relationship with God, and that can't happen if you haven't repented.

Forgive God and the world.

When future author and television host Russell Baker was five years old, his father was suddenly taken to the hospital where he died. Russell said of that time in his autobiography,

For the first time I thought seriously about God. Between sobs I told [the family housekeeper] Bessie that if God could do things like this to people, then God was hateful and I had no more use for Him.

Bessie told me about the peace of Heaven and the joy of being among the angels and the happiness of my father who was already there. The argument failed to quiet my rage.

"God loves us all just like his own children," Bessie said.

"If God loves me, why did he make my father die?"

Bessie said that I would understand someday, but she was only partly right. That afternoon, though I couldn't have phrased it this way then, I decided that God was a lot less interested in people than anybody in Morrisonville was willing to admit. That day I decided that God was not entirely to be trusted.

After that I never cried again with any conviction, nor expected much of anyone's God except indifference, nor loved deeply without fear that it would cost me dearly in pain. At the age of five I had become a skeptic.[3]

Sometimes loss, suffering, and hardship in our lives cause us to doubt the love of God and turn away from him. If this has happened to you, I'm not asking you to minimize what happened, but I am asking you to forgive God and the world. Give up your unhealthy reaction to the harm that has befallen you.

Forgive yourself.

Once you have sought forgiveness from God and from others for neglecting your spirituality, then forgive yourself too. Make an event out of it, something you'll remember like it's the fateful crossing of a river. Say out loud, "I forgive myself for _____."

Do this, and you'll be ready to move past your God regret for good.

God-Ward

I have a truth I need to tell you: You can't find God on your own. Humanity is just not capable of crossing the distance from earth to heaven on its own. But if you seek to find God, he will meet you more than halfway. In fact, he'll come a-running, just like the father in the parable of the lost son.

In other words, although you can't redeem your spirituality regret on your own, God is more than capable of doing it for you. And he will do it through Jesus, who called himself "the way."[4] His life mission was "to seek and to save the lost."[5] He is the path to God. If you choose to follow Jesus, he will take you to the Father.

This way is available to you no matter how long you have been wandering far from God.

Jesus once told another parable about some day laborers who hung out in the local marketplace, hoping an employer would come by to give them some work.[6] It just so happened that a landowner was looking for people to work in his vineyard. For some reason, he made several trips to the marketplace throughout the day, hiring batches of workers at dawn, at 9:00 a.m., at noon, at 3:00 p.m., and even as late as 5:00 p.m. At the end of the work day, he gave all the workers the same pay, regardless of how many hours they had put in.

Again, the symbolism of this story isn't tough to master.

- The landowner = God.
- The workers = people who need to find their way back to God.
- The pay = a relationship with God.

In the parable, some of the earliest-hired workers complained about the seeming unfairness of the pay arrangement. But the landowner wasn't having any of their selfish complaints. He could be lavish in paying the last-hired workers the same wages as the first-hired workers if he wanted to. In the same way, God, through Jesus, gives the lavish gift of his acceptance to people regardless of what point in their lives they come to him.

For you, it might be noon or the midafternoon of your life. Maybe you can even see evening closing in. It doesn't matter. If you have regretted being at a distance from God, it's not too late for the redemption of knowing him through Jesus. You'll have the same reward of his love as anyone who has followed God from early in life.

Trust that God wants to be in a relationship with you even more than you want to be in a relationship with him and that he is in the process of crossing the gap to you. Pray this prayer of redemption:

Redeemer God, I want to believe in you. I want to know you. I want to be close to you. So if you are real, make yourself real to me. Awaken in me the ability to see that you are what's missing in my life. Show me Jesus. Amen.

As you are waiting to feel God's embrace, do all you can to learn about and experience God's love. Read Scripture. Try praying, even if you aren't sure what to say to God. Overcome your fear of rejection by the religious community and start participating in a church. Particularly, I suggest that you get involved in a small group of people who will accept you regardless of where you are on your spiritual journey and help you draw closer to God.

These are all strategies that my friend Martin has employed. His story reminds us that we can find our way back to God at any age.

ON THE RIGHT PATH

Martin was born into a traditional Irish family in northern New Jersey. He was christened at birth, received Holy Communion in the second grade, was confirmed in the eighth grade, and in adulthood considered himself a man of faith. Yet he wasn't truly close to God.

Martin attended church sporadically, mostly on the major religious holidays. He considered it an obligation, not something he looked forward to. "Mostly," he says, "I went out of guilt."

Even so, Martin always tried to live a good life and do the right thing. He has a loving wife, a wonderful daughter, a successful career, a nice home, and some money in the bank.

He says, "I've had my share of disappointments. My mom died in a tragic car accident when I was twenty-five. I went through a divorce at age forty. But I kept an optimistic outlook, worked hard, and generally speaking, things have worked out pretty good thus far."

Nevertheless, Martin began to feel a restlessness inside.

"I'm fifty now," says Martin. "Probably more than halfway done. I've worked hard to get here. Many would say that I've achieved the American dream, and yet there's something missing. There's something *big* missing. There's got to be more to life than just going to school, getting a job, getting married, retiring, and dying."

Martin began to understand that his restlessness was connected to his spirituality, or lack thereof. He was regretting that he wasn't closer to God.

Rather than continuing to recognize something was missing and doing nothing about it, Martin and his wife, Renee, walked through the doors of Community for the first time about two years ago. He hoped he might find what was missing. Today, they're still participating in the church, its ministries, and a small group that means a lot to them.

Martin says, "I still have a long way to go, but I feel that, finally, after a half century of trying it my way, I'm on the right path. The path to filling in the blanks, to answering the unanswered question. The path to finding my way back to God."

Martin's story reminds me that it is never too late to find your way back to God. Just like the workers who came to the vineyard at the end of the day and were paid the same wages as those who were there for the entire day, we are always able to receive God's grace and forgiveness.

You might feel like it's too late. You may have piled regrets upon regrets to the point where you can't imagine a way out of the Sorry Cycle. Let me assure you that it is never too late to find your way back to God.

sibling rivalry
parenting mistakes
estrangement
widowhood
drifted apart loneliness
DIVORCE
miscommunication
BREAKUP betrayal ABUSE
abandonment
neglect separation
unfaithfulness
molestation fighting
immorality
power struggles date rape
unwanted singleness
unhappy marriage
unrequited love
too busy
broken engagement

CHAPTER 7

HEARTS AT RISK

RELATIONSHIP REGRET: "I wish I had loved and been loved better."

If you don't have any relationship regrets, feel free to skip this chapter. But I know you won't.

Because *everybody* has relationship regrets!

Relationships are complicated. We're engaged in them all the time. And they hold vast potential to bring us joy, despair, or just about any other emotion in between. Often we think back and wish we had acted differently in our most important relationships, and just as often we wish others had acted differently toward us. So it's completely unsurprising to me that relationship regrets make up the most common group of regrets.

Researchers at two Illinois universities carried out a survey asking respondents to describe one memorable regret. A total of 47 percent of those regrets centered around relationships.[1] The most frequent response involved romance, with respondents telling a story of a missed love connection. Close behind came family issues, as respondents expressed regret over such things as a family squabble or having been unkind to a sibling as a child. Also showing up in the survey were parenting mistakes and friendship blowups. Yes, we all experience relational regrets.

One other lesson from the survey is that women are more than twice as likely as men to describe relationship regrets. (Men, on the other hand, have more career and finance regrets.) A psychological researcher commented, "These results are in line with the argument that for women relationships with others are more self-defining and more a basis for self-evaluation than they are for men."[2]

But that doesn't mean that relationship regrets are an issue only for females. Psychologist Randi Gunther, who counsels men hurt in dating situations, said, "In my practice, men who cared deeply for the women they lost are just as regretful, if not more so, than women."[3]

You might have regrets deriving from your *birth family:* parents and siblings.

Or from your *extended family:* grandparents, aunts and uncles, cousins, nephews and nieces.

Or from *romance and dating:* crushes, dating partners, lovers, fiancé.

Or from *marriage and parenting:* spouse, kids, in-laws.

Or from *more distant relational bonds:* friends, neighbors, coworkers, acquaintances.

Regardless of the source of your regrets, I'm sure of this: your relational regrets matter greatly to you. You may have been dwelling on them for a long time in a Sorry Cycle. Perhaps you haven't been able to get beyond them—the mistreatment you received as a child seems to have left a permanent scar, or the divorce feels as if it has stolen your future, or your failures as a parent appear to have estranged you from your child for good.

You may have regrets of love missed, love lost, or love spoiled. You keep saying to yourself, "I wish I had loved him better" or "I wish she had loved me better." But I'm here to tell you that there's redemption to be had in this emotionally fraught area of relationship regret.

THE RESILIENCY OF LOVE

Do you remember Donald, the mentor whose self-made failure I described in chapter 1? Donald taught me that ministry is all about relationships, and the fact that he messed up his own relationships doesn't alter the truth of what he taught; it only reminds us that relationships are as hard as they are important.

Inspired by Donald, we call our church Community Christian Church, putting *community* out front, because we believe God really does expect his people to follow him together.

You and I and everybody else were designed as relational beings. Some people are more introverted than others and need more time alone to be re-charged—I get that. But I still believe that all of us crave and need people in our lives. And most of us know that we crave and need other people. But when things go wrong in relationships, we begin to doubt the wisdom of connecting with others. We withdraw. We hesitate. We equivocate. We risked our heart; it got beat up; and we're not so sure we're ready to risk it again.

If you have relationship regrets, I know you're hurting. You may be lonely. You may question whether you can ever trust others again. *Relationships—are they even worth it?* you may be wondering.

The underlying point of this chapter is that, despite whatever has gone wrong in our relationships, we can never be the people that we were meant to be and that we want to be unless we renew our commitment to relationships. We need to be willing to put our bruised hearts out there once again. But next time, we need to approach relationships less by relying on our own impulses and more by trusting in God. The three Rs of *recognize, release,* and *redeem* will set us free to restore old relationships or begin new ones that satisfy our need for love and connectedness.

When a rainstorm strikes, many types of flowers close up and bend over, appearing to be cringing before the onslaught. Sometimes it looks as if they're done for. But when the sunlight comes out, they gradually open their petals, turn toward the light, and begin to grow and thrive once more. That's what can happen to your life on the other side of relationship damage.

Relationship Review

The place to start in healing from relationship regrets is to recognize what happened. Be clear about what it was. If you've been in denial about it or trying to ignore it, admit to yourself that it happened. Then remind yourself that, as rough as it may have been, you can start over. You will love and be loved again.

Remember the three regret buckets.

- Was this a regret of action? *I shouldn't have cheated on my wife. I shouldn't have told my friend's secret after she warned me not to. I shouldn't have teased my daughter so much.*

- Was it a regret of inaction? *I should have paid more attention to my girlfriend. I should have worked less and been more present for my kids. I wish I'd taken the trouble to visit Grandpa at the home when I had the chance. I wish I'd taken more time for the neighbor next door when she so obviously wanted to talk.*

- Was it a regret of reaction? *It was terrible that jerk got me drunk and had sex with me on our first date, but I shouldn't have let it make me feel so badly about myself. I wish I hadn't dwelt so much on how much more successful and athletic my brother is, but at times it made me so angry.*

Identify the effects of the regret on yourself. Have you been dwelling on it in a Sorry Cycle? In your mind, did you perhaps make it out to be a bigger deal than it really was—or on the other hand, a smaller deal than it was? How has it changed you, and how has it changed others, whether directly or indirectly? What has it caused you to do or kept you from doing? What steps have you taken to try to deal with this regret so far, and how successful has that been for you?

There are often powerful emotions involved with this area of regret, so pay special attention to how you're feeling. Put a label on your emotions. Are you feeling wronged? Embarrassed? Rejected? Annoyed? Alienated? Cold? Tense? Lonely? Upset? Fearful? Whatever it is you've been feeling, admit it to yourself. And remember that these feelings don't have to last.

Think about the others involved in the relationship problem. What would their perspective on the situation be? How might they be feeling?

Finally, take whatever lessons from your regret that you can. What does this regret teach you about what you need to do more of, do less of, or do differently in the future? For example, perhaps you have realized that you are too trusting and you need to be more cautious on dates. Or perhaps you need to make more time in your busy schedule for your children. Or perhaps you need to learn to set boundaries in relationships.

PUTTING THE *DYS*– IN *DYSFUNCTION*

So many of our regrets in relationships go back to the family. When you survey your own family history, you may feel shame and disgust at the patterns of dysfunction you see displayed there. Well, let me put things into perspective for you by giving you a quick recap of the relational history of the family of biblical patriarchs: Abraham, Isaac, and Jacob.[4]

First generation. Abraham married his half sister, Sarah. If that's not strange enough, Abraham saved his own skin by letting a foreign ruler take the beautiful Sarah into his harem for a while. Abraham also had a nephew, Lot, who resided with some of the most ungodly people in their region and fathered children by both of his daughters. When Sarah decided she would never have a child, she hooked her husband up with another woman, Hagar, so that Abraham could father a child—Ishmael. Later, when Sarah miraculously gave birth to Isaac, she verbally abused Hagar and Ishmael and talked Abraham into sending those two away without support.

Second generation. Isaac had an arranged marriage with a distant cousin he'd never met, Rebekah. Isaac showed favoritism to their older son, Esau, while Rebekah preferred their younger son, Jacob. At one point Isaac did the same thing his father had done—he protected himself by letting other men sleep with his attractive wife.

Third generation. Jacob conspired with his mother to deceive his father and steal his brother's birthright and blessing, leading to an estrangement with Esau that was never fully healed. Later, Jacob married two sisters, Leah and Rachel, who were relatives of his. His father-in-law, Laban, cheated him, and Rachel in turn stole from Laban. Jacob favored Rachel over Leah, fueling a long-lasting rivalry between the sisters. He also slept with two other women and had children with them. He favored Rachel's two sons, Joseph and Benjamin, over the ten sons he had with the other three women.

Fourth generation. Joseph acted superior to his brothers and relished the special coat his father gave him. In response, the majority of his brothers planned to kill him, then altered their plan and sold him into slavery instead. They deceived their father into thinking Joseph was dead, breaking his heart in the process. One of the brothers, Judah, slept with his daughter-in-law while mistaking her for a prostitute.

Let's add this up, shall we? We've got incest. Polygamy. Endangerment. Adultery. Fornication. Out-of-wedlock birth. Jealousy. Child abuse. Elder abuse. Abandonment. Favoritism. Deception. In-law tension. Sibling rivalry. And prostitution. (Did I leave anything out?)

If you think your family's got dysfunction, consider this one. And this is the family through which God chose to bless the rest of the world!

If God can redeem them, he can most assuredly redeem you too.

The next step toward redemption is release.

"I FORGAVE YOU A LONG TIME AGO"

Danny was relationally careless and paid a high price for it.[5]

He was a successful real estate agent who also founded a small business, along with his grown-up daughter, in Glendale, Arizona. Initially, the future of the business looked bright. Unfortunately, Danny failed to see that two of his employees were working to undermine the business. His daughter, Lauren, kept warning him that the pair was up to no good. But Danny wouldn't listen to her.

When the business was just a few years old, the two disloyal employees left, taking the majority of customers with them, which eventually bankrupted the business. This hurt, but Danny could live with it. More painful to him was the fact that Lauren, in disgust at the way her father had repeatedly ignored her advice, told him that she wanted nothing more to do with him. She moved to a different area, far away from where Danny and his wife, Maureen, were living.

During the first year of the estrangement, Danny wrote letters, made calls, and even visited Lauren to try to bring about a reconciliation. She wasn't having it. So finally he resigned himself to waiting for God to act in the matter.

For three more years Danny didn't see his beloved daughter, his son-in-law, or his granddaughter even once.

For three more years he prayed for reconciliation.

Then one day the phone rang.

The voice on the other end of the call said, "This is James, your son-in-law. Lauren and I want to come see you and Maureen." Lauren had finally let go of the anger she had held on to for so long.

Danny was floored. He managed to blurt out, "Absolutely! Any time!"

On the day selected, Lauren, David, and their daughter all showed up at Danny's house. In tears, Lauren kept saying, "Dad, I am so sorry. I am so, so sorry!"

He told her, "Lauren, I forgave you a long time ago. I have always loved you. I'm sorry too. It's over now."

SETTING THINGS RIGHT

As Danny and Lauren found out, relational regrets require relational release. *Forgiveness* is the key word when it comes to releasing your relational regrets.

Begin by asking yourself the following two questions:

1. *Who hurt me?*

2. *Whom did I hurt?*

Your answers to these questions will tell you whom to offer forgiveness to and whom to seek it from.

The answer to these two questions might be the same. If you're having conflict with someone, you *both* may have said and done something to the other that needs to be forgiven. That's common. And there are few things that reunite two hearts like mutual forgiveness.

Other times, the situation may be more uneven. The fault may truly lay on one side or the other. Either you need to forgive or you need to be forgiven.

Ask forgiveness of others.

Perhaps you did not give yourself fully enough to the people you care about most. Your relational history might be littered with relationships that were sidelined or neglected—or that never developed or matured at all—because you didn't make them a priority. You may have made serious mistakes or even been deliberately unkind.

If you need to, go to someone you hurt, apologize contritely, and ask for forgiveness. Whether or not the other person grants forgiveness, you will have released the burden from your own spirit.

Forgive others.

If someone has hurt you and has not yet apologized, then you need to gently and truthfully let him or her know how you have been hurt. Maybe this person doesn't know what a big deal it was to you or how you are still struggling with it. So approaching this person to talk it over might be the first step toward clearing the air between the two of you and breaking out of your Sorry Cycle.

When you do this, the other person may refuse to apologize. If so, that's unfortunate, but it doesn't prevent you from forgiving the other person in your heart.

Now, it might not always be possible for you to let this person know how you have been hurt. The other person may have died or otherwise be inaccessible to you. Or maybe it wouldn't be safe or wise for you to be in this person's presence. Even then, it's possible to forgive another person in his or her absence.

Write a letter to this person and afterward destroy it. Or go to a quiet place alone and say aloud, "I forgive you for _____."

Go on to make amends or seek reconciliation with the other person, if it is possible and seems wise. But the present goal is to get past your regret. Forgiveness is the priority whether or not reconciliation ever actually occurs.

Ask forgiveness of God.

Perhaps you have broken one of the Ten Commandments by failing to honor your father and mother, by committing adultery, or by coveting something a neighbor has.[6] If you're married, maybe your marriage is characterized, not by love and respect, but by hostility and contempt.[7] If you're a parent, maybe you have been doing what the apostle Paul warned against: embittering your children.[8] There are lots of potential errors in your relationships that don't reflect God's best for you. They not only can harm your relationships with other people but also will create a rupture in your relationship with God.

Confess them all to God. He is faithful to forgive.

Forgive God and the world.

"Why couldn't I be prettier so that guys would notice me?"

"Why didn't God stop it when my uncle crept into my room at night?"

"Why did my wife have to die of cancer and leave me all alone?"

Sometimes there are no answers to our questions about why relational damage has occurred. Yet we're tempted to blame God or the world. Or we're tempted to take shame on ourselves, as if it were our fault. It is not your fault.

We've got to let go of these feelings. Bad things happen because we live in a fallen world. We explained this in chapter 1. And they may make sense in our head, but rational explanations may never heal your broken heart.

Even so, these too are regrets we can move beyond. Ask God to help you release them and let them go.

Forgive yourself.

I've known parents who kept beating themselves up because they spent too much time at work and too little time at home.

I've known people who labeled themselves losers because they spoiled a dating relationship or sunk a marriage through their own foolish choices.

I have no doubt that you could blame yourself for errors you have committed in your relationships. Taking ownership of your errors is appropriate. But dwelling on them does no good.

Once you've done everything you can to clear accounts with God and the people you've hurt, then it's time to cancel the debt with yourself as well. You've got to forgive yourself. That won't change the past, but it will help to open up the future, because you won't be holding yourself back any longer.

THE SOUND OF FORGIVENESS

Loud noises came from behind the closed doors leading to the Egyptian prime minister's reception chamber.[9] The noises sounded like crying or wailing. *Blubbering* might be a better term for it.

A messenger for the Pharaoh happened to be in the prime minister's palace at the time, and he walked straight up to the prime minister's palace steward, who was standing next to a column in the courtyard. The messenger nodded toward the ornate doors of the reception chamber and asked what was going on.

The steward was just as surprised as the messenger about the sounds they were hearing. Zaphenath-Paneah, the prime minister, was usually dignified and self-controlled, exuding an aura of calm confidence as you would expect from the second most powerful man in Egypt. Blubbering was the last thing the steward expected to hear from a room where Zaphenath-Paneah was holding audience.

"I don't know what's going on in there," said the steward. "The prime minister is with some foreign shepherds, more of those people who want to buy our grain stores. This lot have been here before. Why the prime minister should even give a moment of his valuable time to those rough, goat-stinking fellows, I can't imagine."

"Should we take some guards and check on the situation?"

"No," said the steward definitely. "Zaphenath-Paneah was clear to me that he wanted to be left alone with those men."

The blubbering sounds rose again. The messenger and the steward looked at one another, shrugged, and slowly ambled away.

They didn't know, but we know what was going on inside the closed room. Zaphenath-Paneah had revealed himself to his visitors as Joseph, the son of Jacob who had been sold by his brothers into slavery decades earlier. His visitors were these very brothers. Joseph was telling them that he forgave them and would not hurt them.

When he stepped up to Benjamin, an innocent younger brother who had been a mere boy when Joseph lived at home in Canaan, the emotion overcame them. "He threw his arms around his brother Benjamin and wept, and Benjamin embraced him, weeping. And he kissed all his brothers and wept over them."

Undignified blubbering it may have been. But this was the authentic sound of forgiveness dispelling long-standing family conflict. In fact, the dysfunctional mess and the divisions within the patriarchal family that had developed over a period of four generations at last began to heal with this great act of forgiveness.

It was an end and it was a new beginning for God's people.

This is the power of releasing regret by releasing an offender through forgiveness.

STARTING OVER RELATIONALLY

In reassuring his brothers that he truly forgave them, Joseph, aka Zaphenath-Paneah, shared with them the bigger perspective he'd gained on his reaction regret about being sold into slavery. No, what his brothers had done to him wasn't right. And yes, Joseph had been upset about it. He probably entertained revenge fantasies for years. (Take that, Judah! *Pow,* Reuben!) But now he realized that God had been working all along in the midst of this awful situation to put him in a position where he could preserve the chosen family during a period of famine. "You intended to harm me," he told his brothers, "but God intended it for good to accomplish what is now being done, the saving of many lives."[10]

In the midst of relational turmoil and disconnect, it takes faith to believe that God can bring something good out of it. That he can bring redemption. But truly he can.

Perhaps you've known disputing people who have been reconciled or lonely people who have seen their relational lives turned around. You may have had such an experience yourself. So if you're bearing a relational regret, remember that God is a God who works in people's lives to form, preserve, and restore community. Your relational life can begin again.

Pray this prayer for relational redemption:

Redeemer God, you know the pain I feel inside because of a failed relationship. I trust that you are the author of community and the God of new beginnings. Bring healing to my heart. Give me a fresh start in my relational life. Show me how better to love people and have relationships that benefit both me and them. Amen.

As you're waiting for the fullness of redemption to come, take appropriate steps to improve your relational life. The release of forgiveness can be a big part of that. But what else can you do? It depends on the kind of relational problems you've been having. Maybe you need to take a class to help you manage your anger. Maybe you need to switch to a less demanding job so that you have more time for your family.

I don't know what practical steps you need to take, but I bet you do. Usually the problem is not so much one of *knowing* what we need to do as it is *doing* what we need to do. So be bold and take appropriate steps to prepare yourself as you wait expectantly for redemption to come.

God might restore a broken relationship and make it stronger than ever.

Or he might give you new relationships, ones that are better for you than the ones you lost.

One way or another, he has something beautiful in store for you. So don't lose hope. Renew your commitment to love.

LOVE NOTES

Several years ago, I received a call from a church member named Jeff telling me that his seventeen-year-old daughter, Lynlee Bree, had been in an automobile accident and was not expected to survive. I rushed to the hospital to be with Jeff and his wife, Janet. Sadly, just moments before I arrived, Lynlee took her last breath.

Later, as we prepared for the memorial service, I learned something about Jeff's relationship with his daughter that reminds me to never let the worst of someone get the best of me and leave me with regret.

Lynlee was a sweet and kind girl, but—as is true with all teenage girls—there were times when her attitude fell short of charming.

Jeff would be the first to tell you that he was far from a perfect father either. There were plenty of times when he wasn't the dad he wanted to be.

Nevertheless, just about every day Jeff would get up early to be with Lynlee before school and pack her lunch. And every day he would write a note—maybe a poem, a verse, or something else encouraging, even if it was just a smiley face—and put it in her lunch. Then, as she would leave, he would give her a kiss and say good-bye.

One day Lynlee came home from school and asked him, "Daddy, are you mad at me?"

"Well, of course not," said Jeff. "Why would you ask?"

Lynlee said, "You didn't leave me a note in my lunch today. And since you have been leaving me notes so regularly, my girlfriends always ask at lunch, 'What did your dad write today?'"

The next day, Jeff went back to writing the notes.

In preparing for Lynlee's memorial, the family went through the papers and memorabilia in her room. As they did so, they found the notes her dad had put in her lunch before she left for school. She had saved every one of those notes.

Jeff is an imperfect guy who, like most dads of teenage girls, made plenty of mistakes in parenting. But he recognized those regrets, and rather than feeling like a failure and letting those moments define him, he let them go and leveraged the simple act of writing a note to ensure that his daughter knew he loved her.

I don't know about you, but I would love to live my life in such a way that my most memorable interaction with my wife or my friends or my children—the people I love—is a simple expression of God's love through me to them. I'm going to deal with my relationship regrets and do whatever it takes to put my relationships on a better footing.

Made for Relationships

If your relationships are not flourishing, there's a reason why your life is feeling stunted and you're stuck in a Sorry Cycle. You were made for community!

I'm about to go a little theological on you, but stick with me. It applies.

Think of the nature of the triune God: Father, Son, and Holy Spirit have lived together in perfect harmony for all eternity. They are a community, sharing relationships with one another that are fully satisfying for them.

Complete in their interrelationship, the members of the Godhead didn't need anyone else. Yet in the overflow of their love, they created other beings upon whom they could shower their blessings. They created the human race in their own relational image. God's goal for people is that we would live in community with him and with one another, just as he has always been in community with himself.

Just try to imagine the story of the Bible without relationships. You can't do it.

Relational language and ideas are all over the Bible. God calls us his Father. He refers to both the nation of Israel and to the church of Jesus Christ as his bride. Jesus calls his followers his friends and brothers. He identified the two greatest commandments as loving God and loving other people. At the cross he provided the means to heal every discord and bridge every relational gulf so that those who trust in him can be united with God and other believers.

In particular, Scripture describes the church in community terms. The New Testament term *church* means "community," and this community is described as a family and even as a body with Christ as our head. Over and over again, we're told to bear with one another, forgive one another, submit to one another, lift one another's burdens, look to others' interests, comfort one another, pray for one another, be patient with one another, encourage one another, have fellowship with one another, and serve one another. Above all, the hallmark of Christ followers is to be our love. And in the end we can expect to live in the New Jerusalem—in other words, a place where people live closely together.

It's all about relationships!

Put your relationship failures behind you. You can't change what went wrong, but you can deny them the power to hold you back from here on out. Trust God and open your heart to the possibility of the new or renewed relationships he wants to bring your way.

CHAPTER 8

FIT AS CAN BE

HEALTH REGRET: "I wish I had taken better care of myself."

A. J. Jacobs has made a career out of spending a year at a time carrying out a lifestyle experiment and then writing humorously about it. But the only experiment that he claims just about killed him was the year he spent trying to follow all the experts' advice on how to be healthy. He writes about it in a book called *Drop Dead Healthy*.

Dermatologists say you should apply the equivalent of a shot glass full of sunscreen every two to four hours. "I think half of my book advance went into sunscreen," Jacobs said afterward. "I was like a glazed doughnut for most of the year."

Germ eradication was another task. Jacobs said, "My immunologist told me that I should also wipe down all of the remote controls and iPhones in my house because those are just orgies of germs. So that took a lot of time."

He also read that the Danish Safety Council advised people to wear helmets, not just when riding a bicycle, but even when walking around. So he wore a helmet when out visiting friends or grocery shopping. He got a lot of funny looks, but his head was never safer in the produce aisle.

Joking aside, Jacobs admitted he actually did learn some practices that have made his life healthier. But much of the health advice he investigated was so ridiculous or extreme or time consuming that it robbed his mental well-being if not his physical well-being. But I guess, at least, he didn't have any regrets about paying too little attention to his health.[1]

Most of us do.

Perhaps when we were young we were active and fit, but as time goes on, we realize that our body has changed shape in a disconcerting way, we don't have as much energy, and we can't do everything we used to. Most likely not all of it is our fault. If nothing else, there's aging to take into account. But some of it can probably be chalked up to our own neglect. So as we look back, we mutter to ourselves, "I wish I had taken better care of myself."

It's disappointing to realize we're not in good shape or don't like our appearance. But that doesn't mean we're doomed to have a disappointing condition. By accepting where we are and then refusing to stay there, we can begin changing our habits to see greater health and physical well-being.

The number-one purpose in this isn't to impress somebody, meet an artificial goal, or turn ourselves into world-class athletes. It isn't even to feel better and be proud of ourselves, although those are nice benefits. The number-one purpose is to make our health as good as it reasonably can be so that we're better prepared to fulfill God's plan for our lives.

Before I tell how to apply the recognize-release-redeem protocol to health regrets, I want to help you think biblically about your health and physical well-being. You see, if we simply adopt views about the body that are current in our culture, we'll find ourselves tending toward one unhealthy extreme or another. The Bible, by contrast, tells us what *God* thinks about our bodies. He designed the human body, and his view of it is the one that counts.

YOUR BODY MATTERS . . . BUT IT DOESN'T MATTER *THAT MUCH*

It's easy for us to peg our beliefs to ideas or slogans that sound good but aren't really based in the truth.

The apostle Paul addressed one misguided slogan that was popular among the Christians in Corinth during the first century: "Food for the stomach and the stomach for food, and God will destroy them both."[2] In other words, their attitude was, "Who cares what we eat? It's just food. It's got nothing to do with our spiritual lives. Unlike our spirits, our bodies and the food we eat here on earth aren't going to last anyway. So let's eat whatever we feel like."

Like many misguided theological ideas, the slogan popular among the Corinthians has some truth in it. Our bodies really do only last for the duration of one earthly lifetime. From dust we were made and to dust we will return. Paul himself compared the body to a tent and says it is put away when we break our encampment in this world and move on to the next.[3] And despite the fact that Paul was evidently a sports fan (judging by all the athletic analogies in his writings), he once wrote, "Physical training is of some value, but godliness has value for all things, holding promise for both the present life and the life to come."[4]

But Paul wasn't going to put up for one moment with the notion that the body and how we treat it don't matter *at all*.

When we choose to follow Christ, Paul says, our spirits are united with the Holy Spirit. And since we were made as physical-spiritual beings, our physical bodies are involved in our relationship with God too. Paul calls our bodies "temples of the Holy Spirit."[5] Now, what's most important about a temple is the divine presence within it, not the walls and roof and decorations. Nevertheless, the presence of God within us lends dignity and significance to our bodies. "Therefore," Paul concludes, "honor God with your bodies."[6]

Some in our culture today would agree with the Corinthians that there's no eternal value or spiritual significance to our body, and therefore we can do whatever we want with it. If we want to use it for whatever happens to feel good, that's fine. If we want to trash it or neglect it, that's up to us as well. It's just a mortal body, they insist. So what's the big deal?

Others in our culture go to the opposite extreme, making the body out to be more important than it is. I suppose that's not surprising if you start with the idea that there is no God and that nature is all that exists. In that case, our physical life on this earth is all that might really matter to us. What's of supreme value to us is the beauty of the body, the health of the body, the achievements of the body, the pleasures of the body, and the longevity of the body.

This extreme is a mistake too. There truly is a greater life for us beyond this one. While this life matters a lot, the next one matters even more.

We see Paul wrestling with these two competing value propositions when he was in jail and considering the possibility that he might be executed. He asked himself if he would rather go on living or die and go to be with Christ. "To me," he mused in a letter to church members he served, "to live is Christ and to die is gain. If I am to go on living in the body, this will mean fruitful labor for me. Yet what shall I choose? I do not know! I am torn between the two: I desire to depart and be with Christ, which is better by far; but it is more necessary for you that I remain in the body."[7]

In the end Paul desired to go on living and be as productive as he could for as long as the Lord willed. That should be our goal too. Our bodily well-being isn't of ultimate importance, but neither is it of no importance. Our intention should be to make a responsible effort to take care of our body in such a way that we can serve God to the best of our ability however he wants for as long as he wants.

A Checkup

If you're disappointed in the current state of your health, face the problem squarely. It may be your fault, or there may have been causes outside your control that left you in less than perfect health. Either way, coming to terms with your current physical condition is the vital first step toward starting over.

Remember, don't regret your regret, even if it's one that stares back at you in the mirror every day. Embrace your regret because you can learn from it.

Do you have a health regret of action? Examples: *I shouldn't have been so reckless about what I ate and all the weight I gained. If only I hadn't spent so many years stressed out about stuff that doesn't really matter. What a fool I was to snort that first line of coke.*

Do you have a health regret of inaction? Examples: *I wish I had worked out more. It's my fault I haven't been getting enough sleep. I should have been going in for my medical exams regularly.*

Do you have a health regret of reaction? Examples: *I hate that I have this condition, but I shouldn't let it make me so inactive. The injury has changed my life forever, but I shouldn't be blaming God for it.*

To help you in your self-analysis, you may want to get some objective data to assess your physical condition. Have your body mass index (BMI) calculated. Or seek out a personal trainer and request a fitness assessment. Or ask a dietician to evaluate your eating habits. And of course, always consult a physician before changing your diet drastically or beginning a demanding new fitness program.

The point is not to make yourself feel badly about where you are. The point is to establish a baseline.

What can you learn from your self-analysis about what you need to do differently for your health from here on out? Maybe it's already becoming obvious that you need to go on a diet, start an exercise program, or take some other specific step to improve your health.

THE PURGE

After the diagnosis comes the prescription. And for your health regret, the prescribed treatment is this: release. Forgive or receive forgiveness, as appropriate, for whatever brought you to a point of poor health, and then let go of your regret.

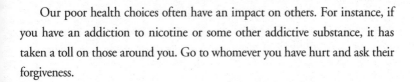

Ask forgiveness of others.

Our poor health choices often have an impact on others. For instance, if you have an addiction to nicotine or some other addictive substance, it has taken a toll on those around you. Go to whomever you have hurt and ask their forgiveness.

Forgive others.

It's possible that others have contributed to your health regret. For example, your parents may have modeled a sedentary lifestyle. Or your spouse may have encouraged poor eating habits. Or a careless coworker may have injured you. And you could be holding on to blame that's corroding your spirit and holding you back from making progress.

Identify who else had a part in your health regret, and how, and then forgive them.

Ask forgiveness of God.

How do you think God would have felt if the priests in charge of the temple in Jerusalem had neglected the place where he had chosen to dwell? Would he have liked it if they had let rubbish accumulate in the temple precincts or allowed the walls to crumble? Of course not.

Neither does he like it when we neglect our own bodies—the temples of the Holy Spirit. He expects us to be good stewards of the health he has given us. If we fail him in this area, it is disappointing to him, and that affects our relationship with him.

So if you know that you have sinned by failing to maintain the body he gave you as well as you should have, ask his forgiveness for that.

Forgive God and the world.

If you're feeling bitter about a health impediment that was nobody's fault, whether a disability, injury, or disease, then you may need to forgive the fallen world you feel is responsible for it. Or perhaps you've been blaming God and you need to forgive him. Either way, at some point in your journey, to move forward you will have to let go of those regrets. And we can move beyond them. Ask God to help you release yours and let them go.

Forgive yourself.

During the process of analyzing your health regret, you identified what you did wrong, whether it was not exercising, overeating, failing to get adequate rest, not seeking medical help earlier, letting stress and anxiety get the better of you, or whatever it may have been. Learn from your mistakes, but don't dwell on them. Let yourself off the hook and move on.

For health regrets, going round and round in the Sorry Cycle is usually accompanied by going round and round in bad health habits. We feel badly about overeating, but then we keep overeating, and that only makes us feel worse. We feel badly about being sedentary, but we still don't hit the gym. We're ashamed of smoking, but we keep lighting up.

Releasing your regrets throws a wrench in the Sorry Cycle and simultaneously makes it possible for you to start acting in a healthier way for your body's sake.

Better an "exer-cycle" than a Sorry Cycle!

SAMMY'S STORY

For the next couple of pages, I'm going to do something a little different. I'm going to turn the book over to my friend Sammy. He's a husband, a father of three, and a guy who is a lot of fun to be around. But he had an area in his life that he regretted greatly. Sammy's story of releasing his health regret and starting over is so powerful that we asked him to tell it in his own words:

Sammy says:

I've been overweight all my life. I guess at some point I just accepted what I thought was the unavoidable reality that I was always going to be overweight. It bothered me. I was mad at myself, maybe even hated myself because of it, but never really enough to make any substantive changes to my lifestyle. Instead, I tried to mask my pain by being the funny guy and letting my personality hide my hurt.

Just over a year ago, I had a pretty traumatic life event that made me stop and face some hard realities about myself. *I was unhealthy.* I was unhealthy spiritually, mentally, and physically. Ironically, I'd spent years telling people that God loved them and wanted them to be healthy in all those areas, but for some reason, in that season of my life, I was confronted by the truth that I wasn't living the way I coached others to live. I needed to change.

So I got to work. I started working on my spiritual life, exploring meaningful ways to encounter God in my personal devotional time. I started seeing a counselor weekly to begin to make a turn in my mental health. And I started getting serious about developing a healthy lifestyle.

The first roadblock I hit was when I realized I had no idea how to eat. I mean, I physically knew how to eat, but I didn't know how to eat in a way that promoted healthy living. As I was trying to learn how and what to eat, a family member suggested a weight-loss program that had worked for her. So I signed up one day and haven't looked back. Through using their app, I've learned how to eat, what portions to eat, what to avoid if I want to lose weight, and how to splurge in a healthy way when I want dessert.

It's been amazing. I lost fifty pounds in the first eight months just by paying attention to what I ate. Once I lost that much weight, I started to figure out that being healthy wasn't just about a number on a scale but it was also about being physically active. Luckily, a good friend of mine is a personal trainer and committed to going to the gym with me three days a week to show me how to use the gym to be active and disciplined in a way that promotes my own health goals.

In the six months since we started working out, I've developed an even more focused discipline about being physically active and paying attention to what and how much I'm eating. I've run my first 5K and plan to run a 10K next year, with the dream of eventually running a half marathon. And the greatest thing is, for the first time, I can chase my kids around the park and they tire out before I do!

As a result of the combined effort of diet and exercise, so far I've lost around ninety pounds. If you would have told me a year ago I could do that, I would have never believed it was possible.

I truly believe that this has been a journey God started me on without my knowing he was even doing it. Somewhere along the way I came to see that the order of my journey toward health wasn't something I decided and then executed, but instead it was directed by God for the greatest impact in my life. The combination of spiritual and mental health and development really helped to give perspective and meaning to my physical health journey.

As I look back on the last year and a half, I've come to realize something—that for most of my life, I've been stuck in a cycle of regret. I've regretted my physical state, my weight, my inactivity, my pants size, but instead of using that as a motivation to change, I let it become a weight that dragged me down and could have killed me.

It wasn't until I started developing spiritually and mentally that I discovered the truth that had been there all along, namely, the truth that I could truly be released from that regret. I realized that I could actually be set free from this horrible world I had created where I doomed myself to an unhealthy lifestyle. In the end I found forgiveness for myself.

Once those things came together for me, the rest just fell into place. I'm not defined by a number, whether it be on a scale, on my pants, or in my head. Instead, I'm valued and loved and made to live an incredible, full, and healthy life. All that's left is for me to embrace it and live.

NEVER TOO EARLY, NEVER TOO LATE

Some authors address health and fitness by talking about willpower. I want to talk about the same thing Sammy did—God's power!

God has all sorts of redemption available for people who hand over their health regrets to him. We can start over in our weight, start over in our strength, start over in our stamina, start over in our body image, start over in so many ways related to our health. Our requirement is to trust God and wait expectantly for the redemption he has for us.

Pray this prayer of redemption:

Redeemer God, I have a deep and painful regret about my health and physical well-being. Help me to start over. Bring about changes, through your power, that convert the hurt and hopelessness in this area of my life into help for me to be the best that I can be. Amen.

Health is one area where God typically partners closely with people to bring something good out of a less-than-ideal situation. He works through the skill of medical professionals, therapists, and trainers. He honors our persistent efforts to improve our fitness. So we need to know that, as God brings about his redemption, he may do it in a collaborative way.

Something else for us to remember is that God designed the human body to function well. So if we give our body what it needs, and avoid the things that harm it, the body will often begin to recover. This, too, is redemption from God. We just have to get out of his way.

Although right now you may look back on your life and say, "I wish I had taken better care of my health," it's not too late for you to make better choices for your fitness and physical well-being. Start over starting today to reach whatever level of health you are able to in order to live the kind of life God wants . . . for as long as possible.

Experts tell us that our bodies respond positively when we start treating them right—at any age. One major research study revealed that exercising regularly in middle age reduces health problems near the end of life.[8] The US Centers for Disease Control and Prevention state, "Older adults, both male and female, can benefit from regular physical activity."[9] A medical journal affirmed, "Weight loss at any age in adulthood is worthwhile because it could yield long-term heart and vascular benefits."[10] Stopping smoking results in health improvement and lowered health risks within weeks or months.[11]

It's not my purpose to tell you *how* to pursue greater health. Instead, I primarily want to encourage you to do it. But I do have some general advice: avoid health and fitness fads and extreme treatments. Like A. J. Jacobs demonstrated, if you go overboard or indulge in quackery, it will eat up your time, steal your money, and possibly not work or at least not stick. Instead, focus on the basics and the perennial advice that's been time tested and proven.

- Avoid overeating.
- Eat a healthy diet with an emphasis on natural foods.
- Get your weight down into the normal range for your height and keep it there.
- Exercise regularly.
- Drink lots of water.
- Get plenty of sleep.
- Manage stress.
- Don't smoke.
- Don't drink too much.
- Only take drugs prescribed by your doctor.
- Get annual physicals with your primary care doctor.

We've all heard this advice so often that we might not even pay attention to it. But so many times I've seen people focus on gimmicks and unproven strategies and wind up getting hurt by it. Before anything else, focus on the basics. Turn them into habits. That might be all you need.

In his bestseller *The Power of Habit,* Charles Duhigg outlines a three-step process to replace poor habits with better ones. He labels the steps *cue, routine,* and *reward.* A cue is something that triggers a behavior; a routine is what you habitually do in response to that trigger; and a reward is what you get out of the habitual behavior that keeps you doing it.[12]

The important thing to note is that we can change our routine in order to harness the power of habit. When a cue triggers us to act, we can choose to do something else that is healthier for us. For example, if lunchtime means to you that it's time go out to eat at a fast-food joint with your coworkers, try packing a healthy lunch instead, eating it at the office, and then asking one of your work friends to spend the rest of the lunch break going for a walk with you. Make this your new habit, and you'll find yourself losing weight and feeling better.

The more urgent your health problem, the more important that you don't put off the first step toward improving your health. Sometimes what we need most is to give ourselves a kick in the pants to get started on change.

The most courageous and compelling message I ever heard in my church was not one I preached. It came from Steve, a father who was speaking at the funeral of his eighteen-year-old daughter, Danielle. She had died from a heroin overdose.

Steve—himself a recovering drug and alcohol addict—stood in front of a packed auditorium and told the crowd, "If you are like me or Danielle and you feel your life spiraling out of control because you are drinking or using and you can't stop; if you hope that there is some power greater than yourself that can help you regain control of your life; let me tell you the absolute truth: you have come to a crossroads, and you are going to make a choice." Steve pointed to the casket holding his girl and said, "You will either choose death, or you will choose to get help!"

Sometimes we've just got to act. We've got to check ourselves into rehab, make the doctor appointment, start the diet, throw out the junk food, put on our running shoes and hit the street . . . or whatever our starting point might be.

There's usually no overnight delivery on God's redemption of our health regrets. Improvement is measured in pounds lost, miles run, weights lifted, laps swum, healthy meals eaten. We don't suddenly arrive at good health. But over time, we can look back and realize that we've made real progress. God has been at work.

You *will* receive some kind of redemption of your health regret. I can say that unequivocally. But I do want to be realistic and affirm that the redemption may not look the way you expect or even want. And if so, that's when you need to remember that the ultimate goal is not to look great in stretch pants, set a new course record for a marathon, or go off your meds. The ultimate goal is to serve and honor God with whatever measure of health he grants.

In Sickness and in Health

Married couples traditionally vow to be faithful to each other "in sickness and in health." Likewise, those of us who make up the bride of Christ (all Christ followers) should be faithful to God regardless of the measure of physical well-being we possess.

One of the most amazing people I ever met was a guy named Charlie Wedemeyer. Growing up, Charlie was an all-state football player and played quarterback at Michigan State. After his college football career, Charlie enjoyed a successful run as a high school football coach. Then Charlie was diagnosed with ALS, or Lou Gehrig's disease. It's a progressive condition that would cause him to lose control of every muscle in his body. He was given one to three years to live.

Charlie and his wife, Lucy, knew that God could cure this disease. They prayed and their family prayed and their friends prayed for God to heal him. Charlie hung on far longer than the doctors expected. But healing didn't come. The disease only got worse.

Even when there was no sign of hope for healing, Charlie and his wife fixed their hope on God. And in the meantime, Charlie kept trying to do some good in this world.

Over the next seven years, Charlie continued to coach high school football—

from a wheelchair! His teams went 78–18–1 and won seven league titles. He coached players who went on to the NFL.

His success as a coach in a wheelchair gave him opportunities to take his story on the road and speak in front of millions of people. What he had to say was so inspiring that it became a best-selling book and an Emmy award–winning movie.

He spoke at our church and this was his message: "Pain and suffering are inevitable, but misery is optional. We have a choice."

Before you write that off as motivational cliché, remember that these words were spoken by a man who seemed to be losing everything. He was losing his health. He was losing his life.

But he didn't lose hope.

Why? Because his hope wasn't just in getting the physical healing he so badly wanted. His hope was in a meaningful life lived in the face of ALS. "Pain is inevitable, misery is optional" were words spoken by a man whose body was so broken that his only means of communicating was to whisper words into his wife's ear so she could speak for him.

Charlie and Lucy put their hope in the one who said, "The one who believes in me will live, even though they die."[13] And in doing so, Charlie gave hope to millions. What is that if not redemptive?

STAYING GREEN

Physical limitations may come our way, and if they do, we can recognize that they give us new ways to be faithful to God and show his power. When we are weak, he is strong.

Nevertheless, we should do our best to maintain our health and fitness. Our goal, as far as it depends on us, should be long-term health. This should be our goal, not just so that we can enjoy comfort and a long life, but also so that we can have long-term productivity and faithfulness to God.

Psalm 92 says,

[The righteous] will still bear fruit in old age,
they will stay fresh and green.[14]

What a beautiful picture of vitality persisting until old age—a fruitful, green tree! And this long-term vitality should be our objective.

Be honest about the health problem you're facing. Hop off the Sorry Cycle. And begin trusting and partnering with God for a healthier future. May you flourish for many years to come.

CHAPTER 9

DOLLARS AND SENSE

FINANCE REGRET: "I wish I had been smarter about money."

Several years ago, the economy was buzzing with wealth. Housing prices were on the rise, the stock market was growing at a record pace, and everyone was looking for a way to make a quick buck. People were so confident in the future that the common wisdom of the day was that, if you didn't have cash on hand, you should invest the equity in your home. "After all," people said, "that's your money anyway."

It was about this time that a good friend began accumulating significant wealth through some obscure but "sure bet" investments. He invited Jon, me, and some friends to put money into a fund that he was starting with some other people. He promised monthly returns that would quickly pay off a person's original investment and eventually deliver a huge payoff.

I even remember him saying to me, "Dave, I am so sure of this, I am urging my mom to invest in this opportunity. If there ever was a no-miss moneymaker, this is it."

As he said this to me, in the back of my mind I could hear my dad's words to me over the years: "If it sounds too good to be true, it's likely too good to be true." But I told myself that this maxim didn't apply in this case.

Our friend was the furthest thing you could imagine from being a salesperson. He was soft spoken and well liked, and he had a track record of honesty and integrity. No one could imagine that the investment he was talking about was anything except the real deal. So Jon and I both borrowed from the equity in our homes and bought into the fund to the tune of $25,000 each.

As you have probably already guessed, Dad was right again. This sure thing *was* too good to be true. Unfortunately, Jon and I didn't figure that out until several years after we had invested. In the end we wound up not merely failing to make a profit but also spending a long time paying off the money we had borrowed against our homes. Meanwhile, our friend and his partners went to jail for fraud.

I guess I should have suspected something was wrong when I learned that Crook was the last name of one of the guys who was heading up the fund. (True story. You can't make that up!)

For the longest time, Jon and I had major regrets over that investment. We felt so stupid. I asked myself over and over, *How in the world could I have fallen for that scam?*

I know I'm not alone in having financial regrets. Many others have blown savings, missed out on a moneymaking opportunity, or put themselves at financial risk. The effects of these money regrets can be long lasting, and so the memory of them can really wear on us.

Nevertheless, it is possible to get past financial regrets, like any other regrets.

If you're hoping this chapter will teach you how to get rich, I'm afraid you'll be disappointed. I'm not even sure that getting rich would be good for you. But I do want to assure you that you can start over in the financial area of your life and become a better money manager. My point in this chapter is that your money is actually God's money, and with his help you can learn to take better care of it, both so that you can provide for yourself and your loved ones and so that you can be generous toward God and others. It's a wonderful thing when you go from being uptight and fearful about your money to feeling secure and content!

Please read the following couple of scenes from an unproduced movie script, and let them prompt you to start looking at your money management from God's perspective.

Bags of Gold

FADE IN:

EXT. FRONT ENTRANCE OF JUDEAN COUNTRY HOME - DAY
(C. A.D. 30)[1]

The Master of the house stands near a small caravan of donkeys, most of them loaded with goods. With him are three male servants. On the ground in front of him lay a pile of rough sacks tied with twine.

> MASTER
>
> I'm not sure when I'll be back, but I'm
> going a far distance and it will take
> a long time. I don't want to lose money
> while I'm gone. So I'm entrusting a sub-
> stantial amount of gold to the three of
> you.

He gives five bags to the first servant, three bags to the second servant, and one bag to the third. The bags clink as he hands them over.

MASTER

Your job while I'm gone is to take that
gold, use it to do business of some
kind—you can choose what kind—and turn
a profit. Remember, it's my gold. Both
the capital and the profit you make belong to me. But of course you can spend
what you need to on expenses and your
own upkeep. I'll expect a careful ac-
counting when I get back. Any questions?

The three servants shake their heads. The Master
mounts his donkey and rides away. After he does so,
the servants open their bags and take out the gold
coins.

SERVANT 1

I already know what I'm going to do with
my gold. Go to Joppa, buy goods off the
ships coming into the harbor, and bring
them back here in wagons to sell in the
village market. I've thought about this
before, and I think it could be very
profitable. What about you two?

SERVANT 2

I'm not sure. But I've always thought
that the east-facing slope of the Master's land would grow grapes. Maybe I'll
buy some vines and put them in there. I

guess I'll have to sleep in a hut to
keep away animals and thieves.

SERVANT 3

What are you two going to such trouble
for? This isn't even our money. You heard
the Master—whatever you make belongs to
him. And besides, who knows if he'll
even come back? The road is dangerous.

SERVANT 1

So, what are you planning to do with
the gold he gave you?

SERVANT 3

Bury it someplace. That way, if he does
come back, I can give it back to him. But
at least I won't have lost any of it by
messing up in investing it. He would hate
that! He only gave me one bag anyway.
That shows you how much he trusts me.

INT. COURTYARD OF THE MASTER'S HOME - DAY (THREE
YEARS LATER)

The Master is sitting on a bench in the shade, eating
from a bowl of figs and dates. The three servants are
standing before him. Meanwhile, in the background,
other servants are carrying goods into the house from
the newly returned caravan outside.

MASTER

I'm ready to hear how you three did in
investing my gold. I hope you have good
news for me.

Servant 1 steps up. He is holding a basket filled with
bags.

SERVANT 1

Master, you gave me five bags of gold
and now I have ten for you.

MASTER

That's excellent! You've proved yourself to
be capable, so you can expect more responsibility in the future. And you'll find
that I reward those who are faithful to
me. (To the second servant) How about you?

Servant 2 steps up. He has a smaller basket contain-
ing bags.

SERVANT 2

I also have doubled your investment,
Master. From two bags to four.

MASTER

That's very good. Just like your friend
here, you'll find that I rely on and take
care of those who have proved themselves

faithful. Step aside now, please. (To the
third servant, who is hanging back) Well,
come on, come on. What have you got?

Servant 3 reluctantly approaches the Master, carrying
a bag stained with soil.

SERVANT 3

Master, I was afraid of what you would
do if I lost your money by speculating
with it unsuccessfully. So I kept it
safe for you. Here is your original bag
of gold.

MASTER

(Angrily) What?! You're lazy, that's what
you are! The least you could have done
is give the gold to bankers so I could
have earned interest on it. (To the
first servant) Here, you. Take this
man's bag of gold.

Servant 1 takes Servant 3's bag and drops it in his
own basket.

MASTER

(To Servant 3) You, I'm afraid, are in
very serious trouble.

FADE OUT

Disclaimer

I expect you recognized one of Jesus's parables in the preceding scenes. I think we can learn a few key truths from this parable that will help us redeem any regrets we have about our finances as well as provide hope for a new financial future.

- *All our money belongs to God.* We're just stewards of it. Whether we spend it on ourselves or give it away to do good work, we should be seeking to please him by our choices.
- *Different people receive different amounts of money from God— and that's okay.* We don't have to be concerned about how many "bags of gold" other people have. We should just be thankful for our own "bags of gold" and take care of them as best we can.
- *God wants us to manage our money effectively.* He gives every one of us the responsibility of doing our best with the money he gives us, and he's watching to see how we make the most of it.
- *More important than the outcome of our money management is our faithfulness in trying to do our best for God.* We may not earn as large a return for God from our money as someone else does, but as long as we do what we can with what we've got, that's a win. God wants to see that we're striving to be obedient and trustworthy.
- *Faithfulness leads to greater responsibility and reward.* It's an honor to be entrusted with God's resources, and it's encouraging to know that our faithfulness can lead to greater rewards on earth and in heaven.

These truths are every bit as valid in the day of exchange-traded funds and hedge funds as they were back when the economy was based on bartering and coin transactions.

Today's investment literature typically offers this disclaimer: "Past performance is no guarantee of future results." In other words, "Even though this investment turned in some good results in the past, and we really want your money for buying in now, we're required by our legal department to warn you that you could lose out."

But you know, if you apply the disclaimer to yourself, the opposite interpretation could be true. Even though your past performance in managing money may not have been stellar, you can do much better in the future!

Perhaps former financial mistakes have put you in a Sorry Cycle. Maybe you've lost confidence in your ability to make good choices about money, and you're not even trying anything different.

Don't let regrets of the past keep you from trying your best with your finances now. Future results may be quite different if you make money decisions based neither on the pull of greed nor the push of fear but instead out of a sincere desire to please God.

Such money stewardship is a responsibility, and yet it is not a heavy one. "My yoke is easy and my burden is light," says Jesus.[2] Your money is God's money. He is with you to guide you and help you in taking care of it. When you do it profitably, you get to share in the thrill of the success with God.

THE DUMB STUFF

"I love money. I love everything about it," said comedian Steve Martin. "I bought some pretty good stuff. Got me a $300 pair of socks. Got a fur sink. An electric dog polisher. A gasoline-powered turtleneck sweater. And, of course, I bought some dumb stuff, too."[3]

Financial regrets may not be the most burning regrets most people have, but they are among the most common kinds of regrets. Almost all of us, when we look back at our history of financial decisions, see some mistakes that are still affecting us today. We say, "I wish I had been smarter about money."

A credit counseling organization polled consumers online, asking them to name their biggest financial regret. The most common response, by far, was habitually overspending (53 percent). In the next four spots were saving too little (18 percent), not saving enough for retirement (14 percent), not buying a house (10 percent), and buying a house (5 percent).[4] Those last two remind us that what's financially smart for one person may be a mistake for somebody else. Or maybe they teach us that human beings are never satisfied!

We can have financial regrets of action. Examples: *I wish I hadn't gone into debt to buy a car that was so much nicer than I need. I wish I hadn't signed up for all those credit cards and sunk my FICO score. I wish I hadn't made investment decisions with my emotions instead of cold logic.*

We can have financial regrets of inaction. Examples: *I wish I'd built up an emergency fund. I wish I'd lived by a budget. I wish I'd bought a house instead of paying rent all those years. I wish I'd taken advantage of the employee benefits my company offered. I wish I'd started saving for retirement a long time ago.*

We can have financial regrets of reaction. Examples: *I wish that my parents had modeled better money management and that I hadn't followed in their footsteps in this area. I wish my friend had never given me that bad investment tip—and I wish I hadn't gone along with it like an idiot.*

What are your financial regrets? Be as clear and specific as you can in identifying them. Be sure to think also about what these regrets have done to you mentally, emotionally, and spiritually. Then ask yourself, *What do my financial regrets teach me about myself, and how do I need to handle money differently in the future?*

Money management is a skill, and like any skill, you can hone it if you're constantly learning from the feedback you get from your past choices. For example, have you examined your underlying assumptions about money?

Brad Klontz, an expert in financial psychology, has identified four "money scripts," or unconscious belief systems that affect how people approach money:[5]

1. *Money avoidance*—believing that money is bad or you don't deserve money.

2. *Money worship*—thinking that having more money will solve all your problems and give you happiness.

3. *Money status*—looking to money to set you apart from other people.

4. *Money vigilance*—being unusually watchful over and worried about your money.

All four of these money scripts can lead to poor financial decisions. Do your financial regrets reveal that you have embraced one of these beliefs?

Mining your regrets for what they can teach you will help you move to the best financial belief system of all:

Money stewardship—knowing that your money belongs to God and that he will help you manage it well for his purposes.

CUTTING YOUR LOSSES

When it comes to financial regrets, it can be tempting to move directly from identifying our past mistakes to trying a new approach to managing our money. But in this area as much as any other, it's crucial that we take the time to release our regrets. Because if we don't, the dead hand of the past will reach out and interfere with our attempts to manage our money better. We'll fall back into old, bad habits when what we want are new, better ones.

Releasing regrets gives us a fresh foundation to build on.

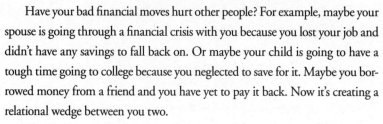

Ask forgiveness of others.

Have your bad financial moves hurt other people? For example, maybe your spouse is going through a financial crisis with you because you lost your job and didn't have any savings to fall back on. Or maybe your child is going to have a tough time going to college because you neglected to save for it. Maybe you borrowed money from a friend and you have yet to pay it back. Now it's creating a relational wedge between you two.

If you've hurt others, ask their forgiveness.

Forgive others.

Have other people contributed to your money problems? Maybe a partner took advantage of you in a business deal. Or maybe a tax advisor steered you wrong, and now you owe a whopping IRS bill.

In order to move on, you need to forgive them.

Ask forgiveness of God.

Have some of your money-related choices been sins, disrupting your relationship with God? This could be the case, for example, if you stole money or ignored the Bible's plea to be generous and not greedy.

If you've sinned, ask God's forgiveness. He's eager to give it and restore the relationship.

Forgive God and the world.

Have some of the problems you've seen in your financial life been the results simply of living in a fallen world where things naturally go wrong? Perhaps a stock market decline has moved retirement out of reach for the time being. Or maybe a housing downturn has put you underwater on your mortgage. Maybe you were the victim of corporate downsizing.

These forces were out of your control. There's no point in blaming the world or God. Forgive these circumstances.

Forgive yourself.

Have you made some foolish financial moves? I know the answer to this question is yes. (I say that in all sympathy. Remember the home equity I chucked in a bad investment?) So most importantly, when it comes to financial regrets, forgive yourself.

Whatever it was that you did or didn't do that left you in a financial mess, don't make it out to be worse than it was. Most likely, it was a common mistake. And for every mistake that you made, you may have made a lot of good choices. In any case, it doesn't pay to hold on to this regret. Tell yourself that it's over and done with. You've already started to turn it to your advantage by learning from it, and now you're going to let it go.

Sometimes people who have made a bad investment are tempted to hang on to it too long. Wiser investors might urge them to sell out, cut their losses, and try again. Well, financial regret is a bad investment, a real dog. Going round and round with it in a Sorry Cycle will only tie up your emotional capital. Sell the dog! Get rid of it now.

Release it.

Climbing Out of the Hole

A young man named Thomas got married, and he and his wife went on a spending spree. After just a few months, they took stock of their financial situation. Thomas reported, "My wife and I had two new cars, lots of shiny things, and had pursued purchasing our first home." After closing on their home, they found themselves $310,000 in debt. Thomas said, "I was left shell-shocked by my own reckless pursuits." He and his wife decided to make some changes. Their goal was to become debt free.[6]

First, they paid off a credit card bill and cut up the card. Then they paid off some bills they had racked up with landscaping and modifications to their house. "Within a span of a few months," Thomas said, "all of our smaller debts were gone. All that we had left were two cars and an enormous mortgage."

Here they got lucky. Or actually, *blessed* would be a better word for it. Sales of one of the products Thomas created for his business began to take off. He was able to increase the salary he allotted to himself from his business. The extra money came in handy as the couple continued to whittle away at their debt.

Thomas said, "I traded in my new car for a nice but slightly used older car to reduce the amount of payments I had. Along with really sticking to our budget and being intense about paying off our debt, we had both cars paid in full. . . . At this point, we only had the house left to go."

Even though Thomas's income was growing, he and his wife had the self-discipline to actually spend *less* so that they could put more in savings.

"Every quarter," he said, "we would take out a lump sum and put it straight towards the mortgage. We didn't blink or think twice—that is exactly what the money was for, and that is exactly where it went."

Three and a half years after they decided to attack their financial problem, the couple had retired their mortgage and paid off their debt—all $310,000 of it.

Thomas reflected, "Was it easy? No. I'm convinced not many things in life worth doing are easy, but our dependence on God, the character development and the relationship bonding created by this entire process is something money cannot and will not buy."

READY FOR MORE

Thomas and his wife are examples of the truth that God can redeem our financial mistakes and make us better money managers. If you have released your financial regrets, he will give *you* redemption too! Trust him and wait with expectancy for the beautiful thing he will bring out of the financial wreckage in your life.

Again, I'm not saying you'll become rich. But even going from having too little to having enough is a huge win. It will feel like the difference between bondage and freedom.

Along the way, you may have other types of less-tangible redemption. I've known people who, while working through financial problems, have grown in compassion for the poor, become less greedy and materialistic, and developed a persistent attitude of gratitude.

If you are ready for God to redeem your financial regrets, pray a prayer like this:

Redeemer God, you know the mistakes I've made with money in the past. I've dealt with them and put them behind me. Now I pray that you will provide generously for me and help me to manage more wisely whatever you give me from here on out. Amen.

As you wait for redemption, commit to being a better steward of the financial resources God places in your hands. Find ways to prepare yourself to be a partner in the financial redemption God is going to send your way. Here are some tips to get you started:

- *Educate yourself about money management.* Isn't it interesting that we learn about math, English, biology, and all kinds of other subjects in school . . . but not about how to handle our money? Correct this oversight. Subscribe to a personal finance magazine. Read books about money management or investment. Find blogs that offer sound advice.
- *Get help.* Ask advice of someone whose financial acumen you respect. Check out the resources of a Christian financial ministry. Hire a financial professional, such as an accountant, a financial adviser, or an investment broker. Join an investing club. Track your finances using an online tool or bookkeeping software.
- *Do the no-brainers.* For example, if you've been spending more than you earn, cut your expenses so that you can create some margin in your budget. If you have debt on a high-interest credit card, start paying it off right away. If you don't have an emergency fund, stash cash away diligently until you have the equivalent of at least three months of living expenses. If your company matches employee contributions to a retirement account, start contributing to your account every month so that you can snag this free money.

The Master in Jesus's parable said to the two faithful servants, "You have been faithful with a few things; I will put you in charge of many things."[7] So start now to learn the skills of money stewardship so that you can be successful with both the relatively small amounts of God's money you have right now and the larger amounts you may have in the future.

And there's still one more aspect of being a good steward. That's being generous to God's work and to others as God has been generous to you. You don't have to wait until you're wealthy to be a giver. Like reinvesting profits in a business, you can pour some of your money—regardless of how big or small your income is—back into the kingdom of God.

So many people think generosity is something God wants from you. Generosity is not something God wants *from* you; it is something God wants *for* you. It's a simple practice that can help you not just start over after a regret but also live on a higher plane of significance for the rest of your life.

My challenge for you is this: Give away a percentage of your income regularly. Increase the percentage every year, and watch how God uses your generosity to change the world and change you.

AUDIT WORTHY

My friend Jim was audited by the IRS eleven out of twelve years on his charitable giving, because they wanted him to prove he'd really given as much as he indicated on his tax return. It was such a large portion of his small income that they figured he had to be exaggerating his charitable contributions.

Early in their marriage, Jim and his wife, Sandy, decided to give away 10 percent of their relatively small income. That's when they made a commitment to increase the percentage they gave away every year. Some years they increased their generosity by 1 percent; other years they increased it by 5 percent. And now they have been giving away more than 50 percent of their income for decades.

When I first learned of their practice, the skeptic in me assumed Jim and Sandy had some hidden wealth. I knew he was a college professor at a small school in East Texas (not exactly a big moneymaking profession), but I figured he must have had other sources of income that made their giving possible. After further investigation, I learned this was not the case. Jim and Sandy were far from wealthy—or should I say, they were not wealthy in the way we typically think of wealth. Their combined salary was never more than $75,000 in a single year.

Jim will be the first to tell you that generosity didn't always come easy. There were economic downturns, unexpected expenses, and plenty of bills to pay, including sending three kids to college. But he will also tell you that, amazingly, God always provided what they needed. And looking back, he doesn't regret living a life of generosity.

You won't regret generosity either. It's a part of the joy of being a good steward of the money God has entrusted to you.

Put the past behind you and start over today as a money manager for God.

CHAPTER 10

MY WHY

PURPOSE REGRET: "I wish I had given my life to a big cause."

The same year I finished college, my Aunt Elayne started going to college. I thought it was such a cool thing for her to do at her age. From my perspective, she was practically ancient—forty-three!

Ever since childhood, Aunt Elayne had intended to go to college. But then she married my uncle right out of high school, worked a job to supplement his income from their farm, and then became a stay-at-home mom raising three kids. She loved her life on the farm with her active family, but she always harbored a regret that she'd never gone to college. She craved a challenging professional career of her own.

Finally she decided not to put off the first step of enrolling at college any longer. "One day it dawned on me," she said, "that the 'baby' was ten years old and the mom was forty-three, so if I was ever going to college, it had to be now."

She drove to a nearby college, laid some money on the counter, and signed up for a couple of courses.

At first she felt embarrassed about sitting in classrooms with students (and sometimes professors) who were much younger than her. But then one day she heard a professor use a word that was new to her—*symbiotic*. As soon as she could, she looked up the word's definition. It felt so good to be learning something new! "When I discovered what it meant," she said, "I was as excited as if I had been given a new recipe for hot rolls. That was the day I quit worrying about the college kids viewing me as old and taking up space."

Not only did Aunt Elayne earn her bachelor's degree, but she went on to complete a master's degree at age fifty. For years she taught world geography and political science for her undergraduate alma mater—and loved it.

What I love about Aunt Elayne's story is that she did not regret her regrets. Instead she saw her regrets as an opportunity to start over. She had a dream about having a career that would be fulfilling to her and helpful to others, and although she had good reasons for setting that dream aside for a while, she eventually pursued it.

Regrets related to education—not going to college, choosing the wrong major, not working hard enough at schoolwork, and so on—are among the most common. About one out of every six respondents to a survey cited an education choice as their most serious regret. Equally common are regrets related to career, such as choosing an uninteresting career or going into a line of work that does not pay enough.[1]

I think these two regret areas—education and career—are connected. Many of us don't have fulfilling work lives, and we think that if we had done our education differently, we would have been better positioned for a career that would have been more satisfying to us.

But let's dive even deeper into human motivation than that. I think people citing these kinds of regrets are really yearning for *significance*.

We all want to have a purpose in life. We crave a goal that provides us with an organizing principle for our lives. We want our days to count, not just pass. We want to believe that our labor has meaning. We want to make a lasting mark on the world as we give ourselves to a cause bigger than ourselves.

Sometimes this significance comes from our work—it's great when we're not just putting in time on the job to pay our bills but rather we see our career as a calling. But then again, our purpose might not have anything to do with our paid labor. For some people, raising great kids is a cause that gets them fired up. For others, volunteering their spare time with a nonprofit provides a sense of fulfillment. For still others, doing creative work, such as painting or writing songs, satisfies an irrepressible creative urge.

Does any of this stir up a familiar sense of longing within you?

Perhaps sometimes you look at your life and think, *What's the point? What reason do I have to get up in the morning? None of this really matters.*

Maybe you wish you had made different choices in the past so that you could be doing something important in your life.

If so, it's not too late!

Like my Aunt Elayne, you can make a change in your life that gets you doing something that suits the unique gifting you were born with and fulfills the yearning you have inside to do something that matters. And more than that, I believe that if you look to God, he will lead you into some kind of significant work. He will make it bigger than you ever imagined by tying it to his own cosmic purposes.

Let's think about how we ought to be spending our time.

SPEED VERSUS VELOCITY

When we think of velocity, we typically think it's the same thing as speed. But actually, velocity is about speed *and* direction. (Look it up.) We confuse speed with velocity at our peril.

Jimmy Deland was by far the best athlete on my junior high basketball team. But I will never forget the time Jimmy stole the ball at half court and sailed toward the basket for an uncontested layup. The ball dropped through the hoop. There was only one problem: Jimmy shot at the wrong basket!

Jimmy didn't need speed. He had that. He needed velocity—speed with direction, the right direction.

Lots of us have speed in our lives. We're so busy that it seems like we could hardly add one more thing to our day! We rely on our calendar apps to keep us on task throughout the day. We check e-mail on the sly in the middle of meetings. We put on makeup in the car. (Not me personally—I want to make that clear.) We try to cram the greatest number of activities into the finite number of hours allotted to us, and at the end of the day we're exhausted.

But what happens when we have a rare moment to reflect on our lives? Do we feel a sense of satisfaction in valuable work well done, or do we start to question whether we're getting anywhere at all?

Busyness can never manufacture a purpose that isn't already there. Busyness may, however, be the result of having a purpose.

I've been more fortunate in this area of life purpose than many. In one research study, 75 percent of Americans said they did not have, or at least were not sure they had, a satisfying life purpose.[2] I'm thankful to be a part of the 25 percent who do know their purpose. Since I was a youth, I've known my calling is to start and lead churches that help people find their way back to God.

In fulfilling my purpose, I keep my days packed. There's always another message to prepare, another meeting to attend, another conference to organize. I tend to be a high-energy, outgoing person, so I don't shrink from having a lot of demands on my time. But still, I'll be honest with you, it can take me to my limits. I don't know what I'd do without my wife, my assistant, my brother, and others who keep me sane and focused.

But here's the thing: I know it's all for a reason. Of course I have to reevaluate sometimes to make sure I'm not committing to activities that aren't really necessary. But for the most part, I'm confident that what I fill my days with is helping me to fulfill my life's purpose. So I can bear my busyness, even rejoice in it.

Busyness that feels pointless is pure misery. Busyness for a reason that you completely buy into is okay. Because then you're not on a treadmill—you're running to get somewhere.

Redeem your regret regarding purpose and you'll redeem your busyness too.

We need velocity in our lives, not mere speed. We need to shoot the arrow of our lives toward a target. And for that to happen, we need to get past our regret.

THE CAUSES OF CAUSELESSNESS

Mark Twain said, "The two most important days in your life are the day you are born and the day you find out why." We begin to figure this out by examining the regrets regarding purpose we've experienced so far in our lives.

When we have a *purpose regret,* it's easy to be vague about it. We can say, "I wish I had given my life to a big cause" and leave it at that. But it's important to drill down further and get specific about the dissatisfaction we're feeling. The only way we'll be able to find the specific calling for our life today is if we identify our specific purpose regret from the past.

Do you have a purpose regret of action? Examples: *I wish I hadn't chosen a safe career over a challenging one. I wish I hadn't focused on making money so much instead of doing something that helps others.*

Do you have a purpose regret of inaction? Examples: *I wish I had applied for grad school. I wish I had started that business I had a vision for. I wish I had volunteered my spare time instead of wasting it.*

Do you have a purpose regret of reaction? Examples: *I wish I hadn't let my high school guidance counselor talk me out of applying to college. I wish I hadn't let my health problems prevent me from going overseas with the Peace Corps.*

When it comes to purpose in life, inaction regrets are usually the most common. We look back and we see that we failed to do something that could have led to bigger impact. But any or all three types of regrets might be feeding into your sense that you haven't yet accomplished as much in life as you could have.

Once you've identified your purpose regret clearly, think about how it has affected you. For example, a lack of purpose often causes us to feel emotions such as apathy, lethargy, disillusionment, disappointment, and even self-loathing.

We might have trouble establishing priorities, making decisions, or knowing what to keep in our lives and what to get rid of. A lot of people with depression and other health problems, I suspect, would be doing better if they had a rousing purpose in life.

How have you dealt with your regret?

Some people who lack purpose in life ride the Sorry Cycle. They keep dwelling on the fact that somewhere along the line they failed to make a choice that would have given them a more meaningful life. If only, if only, if only . . .

But I actually think it's more common for people who lack purpose to go in the opposite direction and unconsciously practice distraction and suppression strategies. It hurts to think about the fact that they're just living day to day without any important goals, so they divert their thoughts from what's missing. It's not hard to do. After all, while their everyday lives might be unfulfilling, at least they can be engrossing. So they kill time. They just waste it on stuff that will pass the time.

The idea of "killing time" kills me! Time is way too precious. We should be making the most of our time, not trying to get it to pass more quickly.

Instead of reacting inappropriately to your lack of life purpose, take a fresh look at where you've gone wrong in the past and think about what you can learn from it. What unhelpful tendencies in yourself do you need to resist? What unrealized potential within yourself could you nurture? What enduring patterns of desire do you detect?

You can't go back and undo the past, but you still have precious gifts to offer the world.

LEAVING IT IN THE PAST

Purpose regrets can be deeply held. We hold on to other regrets too, but they tend to be about *parts* of our lives. A lack of purpose calls into question the value of the *whole* of our lives. And the longer we put off dealing with this regret, the more massive the cost.

We've got to flush away our purpose regrets and start again. We've got to get rid of all that guilt and regret. We've got to release it.

Ask forgiveness of others.

Having a lack of purpose negatively affects not only you; through you, it also negatively impacts those closest to you. For example, if you have been wasting time, being indecisive, or acting apathetic and lethargic, that has been tough on the people closest to you, such as your loved ones and coworkers, wouldn't you say?

Apologize to them and ask for their forgiveness.

Forgive others.

Maybe along the way someone discouraged you or held you back from something meaningful you might have accomplished. For example, maybe when you were younger you were told you would never amount to anything, and because you absorbed that opinion, it prevented you from taking risks or attempting big things. Maybe a boss withheld responsibility from you when you were raring to go on a new venture. This is sad when it happens, but it doesn't have to be insurmountable. You can let it go.

If others have contributed to the absence of purpose in your life, forgive them.

Ask forgiveness of God.

Jesus knocked Saul of Tarsus (later known as Paul) off a horse with a flash of light when calling him to be an apostle.[3] We may not ever have quite so obvious and definitive a call from God. Nevertheless, "we are God's handiwork, created in Christ Jesus to do good works, which God prepared in advance for us to do."[4] So if you have been resisting a call of God to some form of *good works,* that's disobedience. It disappoints God and negatively impacts your relationship with him. Confess and ask forgiveness.

Forgive God and the world.

Poverty might have forced you to go to work right out of high school instead of attending college. The onset of a chronic disease might have interfered with your plan to move to the Philippines and work with orphans. In different ways, circumstances that simply come from this world being a hostile place could have made it more difficult for you to live a life of purpose. That's tough to deal with. Yet holding on to a grudge against impersonal realities or blaming God is just going to keep you locked up in insignificance.

You need to set aside your bitterness if you want to move on.

Forgive yourself.

Most of the blame for our failure to attach to a big cause usually routes back to our own doorstep. But the only thing more purposeless than having a purposeless life is to keep beating yourself up for being purposeless. (Follow that?)

If God and others have forgiven you, you can forgive yourself and move on. Let me get you started: "I forgive myself for . . ."

JUST A SHEPHERD

Moses had three distinct phases of life. Nearly everybody knows the iconic phase 3: Moses as an old man leading the Hebrews out of Egypt and then through a lengthy period in the wilderness, where he received the Ten Commandments. Many people remember phase 1 as well: Moses as a Hebrew baby plucked from the Nile River by an Egyptian princess and raised in the royal household. Rarely, however, do we think about phase 2, when for many years Moses was a shepherd living in the desert area of Midian, far from anything big that was going on in his day. Yet, if we have purpose regrets, it's this phase-2 Moses we should be able to relate to the most.

Picture a middle-aged Moses leading his sheep from one patch of scanty vegetation to another at the base of a mountain in the Sinai wilderness.[5] The work is mindless and monotonous. There's little of interest to look at, no one to talk to. Moses takes a seat on a rock and thinks.

I wonder, does he recall his upbringing, when he was given an education and opportunities that few in his day could even contemplate? When he was a youth, he must have thought he was headed for a life of power and influence in Egyptian society. But now? Moses only has to look around him to see the contrast. Shaggy, stinking herd animals are his only charge. He has a wife and two sons in Midian, and he smiles when he thinks of them, but they hardly alleviate his sense of professional insignificance.

I can also imagine that Moses thinks back to the time when his one chance of doing something really important for God came to a quick end. Back then, he'd been a young man with deeply divided loyalties, because his own people were downtrodden slaves and yet he had been raised among the slaves' owners. His anger had flared up when he saw an Egyptian beating a Hebrew slave, and he'd struck and killed the offender. Perhaps he had the stirring thought that this could be the beginning of a career as leader of the revolt of God's people in Egypt. Who was better placed than he to be their deliverer? Yet the reaction he got from his fellow Hebrews the next day brought a swift halt to any such imaginings. They said, "You're not the boss of us." And soon thereafter Moses fled to Midian. To the life of a shepherd.

For many years after moving to Midian, I imagine, Moses probably regretted acutely the paltriness of his new life. After many years of exile, however, maybe he doesn't even daydream much anymore about doing something important. If ever that were possible, the time has passed. "I'm just a shepherd now," he sighs to himself at the conclusion of indulging his youthful memories.

Then he sees a light in the distance. He shades his eyes with his forearm to get a better look. Is that a bush on fire?

Missional Me

Moses had tried to turn himself into a deliverer of his people as a young man in phase 1, but that failed attempt didn't go far because it wasn't the right time and he wasn't going about it in the right way. Self-engineered redemption has a way of falling apart in the most humiliating manner. But when God was ready to redeem Moses's purpose regret, success finally lay at hand.

If you have admitted to yourself that you haven't accomplished as much of lasting significance as you feel you could and should, and if you have released your regret and are ready to start over, then you're ready to trust God for the redemption he desires to bring about in his own time and in his own way.

Purpose redemption isn't just a matter of fulfilling your potential. I'm not talking about some kind of trendy self-actualization or becoming your "greatest self." I'm talking about doing *more* than you're capable of, because "it is God who works in you to will and to act in order to fulfill his good purpose."[6] And he is "able to do immeasurably more than all we ask or imagine, according to his power that is at work within us."[7]

Now let's be clear about something. Is having a calling or a mission just about professional ministry? No. Leading a church is a calling, and so is being a businessperson who creates jobs and produces goods or services that improve the lot of humanity. Being a worship leader is a calling, and so is swinging a hammer with Habitat for Humanity, collecting clothes for a homeless shelter, and tutoring a high schooler who's reading at a fifth-grade level.

God will open your mind to the beauty and diversity of the redemption he offers. And he'll lead you to your own particular place in it.

Pray this prayer of redemption:

Redeemer God, today I renew my desire to accomplish something signifi- cant in this world. Bring me out of my time of aimlessness and discourage- ment. Help me to accomplish the good work that you have prepared for me to do. Empower me to accomplish what only you can imagine. Amen.

As you are waiting for God to answer your prayer, begin to make preparations that may put you in place for God to use you. My Aunt Elayne would have never taught a single college course if she hadn't made a decision to get a college education. I wouldn't be a pastor if I hadn't taken the time to learn about ministry. You too need to lay the groundwork for a future life of significance. Even if the redemption God brings about is utterly inconceivable to you now, he will use the preparations you have made.

- *Evaluate your personal wiring.* You've already started this process by recognizing and interrogating your regret. Go on to consider your gifts and passions, and start thinking about where they intersect. Be grateful for what you have to offer. Think about how you can develop your potential.

- *Reorganize your life, if necessary, to free up time and other resources.* For example, downsize your lifestyle so that you don't have to work so many hours and are free to do the volunteering your heart yearns for. Consider commitments you may need to say no to in order to say yes to more significant work.

- *Start small.* Look for simple opportunities to give yourself in a big way to the people and places you encounter every day. Build from there.

- *Be willing to make changes.* Start thinking about going back to school, changing jobs, starting a business, networking with a different crowd, or volunteering for a program that interests you.

- *Seek confirmation.* Ask those you trust to tell you what they think you have to offer the world. They might have a clearer picture of what you're suited for than you do yourself.

Remember, individual life purpose varies a lot from person to person. It might be raising a family or starting a business that offers a product or service no one else has put on the market. You may volunteer for a nonprofit, pursue political involvement, or start a social justice ministry.

These big causes aren't all necessarily big in the eyes of others. But they are big to us because we know that they would call for the best within us and convert our gifting into high-impact results.

WHEN PAY IS A BONUS

My youngest son's science teacher was a man named Arnoush Javaherian (people call him "Java"). Recently, I heard him tell his story of searching to find something meaningful to do with this life. It was inspiring to me and everyone else who heard it.

Some years earlier, Java had a well-paying job, but he was in a rut. One day he woke up and said to himself, *I hate my job, I don't like where I am in life right now, and I don't want to go to work today.* He decided to do something about it.

He had known for a long time that his passion was teaching. Years prior, a coach had told him that he ought to be a teacher. Experiences along the way in his life had confirmed this viewpoint. Now Java was ready to pursue this goal.

He applied to a graduate school, where he studied both science and education. It took him three and a half years, but he finally received his education degree.

Then he applied for jobs in thirty-one school districts in the Chicago area. The first school to call him in for an interview was the one my children attend. After talking for a few moments, the principal started to offer him a job.

Without waiting to think it over or even hear the principal out, Java said, "Yes."

"But I haven't made you a salary offer yet," objected the principal.

Java stuck out his hand to shake on the agreement. He said, "I accept whatever you offer. It is a privilege to have this role as a teacher, and I will do it for whatever you will pay me."

I love that!

Today, Java calls teaching his "dream job" and says he is "the happiest person alive." My son can attest to the fact that Java is a great teacher who knows how to get kids interested in science.

I wouldn't be a bit surprised if they also learn something from him about following their God-given passions and choosing to do what they love—even if they don't know what it's going to pay!

Don't Quit

Before I get to my conclusion on this topic, I need to give you some encouragement counterbalanced by a caution.

Like Java's happiness in being a teacher, giving yourself to a calling or cause will probably make you feel good. It will reverse a lot of the negative effects that you identified when you examined your regret. Instead of being indecisive, you'll know what you want. Instead of acting lethargic, you'll be energized. Instead of feeling down and discouraged, you'll enjoy what you're doing and feel optimistic about the future.

Psychological researchers have shown that having a purpose in life is associated with healthy aging and increased longevity. And it doesn't seem to matter when you discover and begin to pursue your life purpose. After looking at longitudinal data, the researchers said, "Having a purpose in life appears to widely buffer against mortality risk across the adult years."[8] That means if you have a reason to live, you will actually live longer!

Other research has shown that "having purpose and meaning in life increases overall well-being and life satisfaction, improves mental and physical health, enhances resiliency, enhances self-esteem, and decreases the chance of depression."[9]

If you experience those kinds of benefits from having a life purpose, I'm really happy for you!

But—and here comes my caution—purpose isn't a pill you take to make you feel good and have a happier, longer life. It is a responsibility you accept and carry through to its conclusion. And though living out a purpose almost always gives us a sense of satisfaction on a deep level, it doesn't guarantee an easy life.

I could give you all kinds of examples from Scripture, but let's skip right to the most important one—Jesus. He spent three years of homeless wandering in and around Israel, laboring to the point of exhaustion and enduring a growing pressure of opposition. Then, at the age of only thirty-three or thereabouts, he let himself be crucified. He didn't just *give himself* to a cause; he *gave himself up* for a cause. But none of that means he had missed his calling. He hadn't failed. To the contrary. He was able to say "It is finished" on the cross because he had completed his mission to the utter satisfaction of his heavenly Father.[10]

When God redeems your regret regarding purpose, pursue your calling not because it is fun but because it is right. And when times get tough, don't quit. Keep going until you too can say, "It is finished."

What can keep you going?

If you'll take one giant step back from the issues surrounding your own purpose, I'd like to show you the big picture. This oughta blow your mind.

THE EPIC TO END ALL EPICS

Most of us are attracted to dramatic stories with great sweep and movement. We read thick novels involving large casts of characters and plenty of action, culminating in danger and possibility. We love movies that are epic in scope and consequence. The hero is so valorous, and the villain is so degraded. It's all so big and stirring!

Now imagine there were a plot line that stretched from the beginning of human history to the end. Imagine there were a plan under way, one with the greatest possible consequences, as Good battles Evil across every continent and from one century to the next. Imagine that the conclusion will establish the forces of good forever as it changes the very nature of human reality.

This is really happening.

God is building a kingdom—an extension of his rule and influence—all over the world and in every ethnic group throughout history. He does it by winning over individuals one by one to his way of love through his Son, Jesus. He also does it through acts of redemption in human culture that little by little convert darkness to light, evil to good.

This is God's vast cosmic plan "to reconcile to himself all things, whether things on earth or things in heaven."[11] And we can have a part in it whenever we contribute, even in a small way, to the building of his kingdom. *Sacred* and *secular* are just words if whatever we are doing serves God's purposes. Any career can be a calling if it offers good for humanity. Even an avocation can be a vocation.

This is why our purpose regrets are so piercing. Deep down, we know we were meant for more than just getting ourselves through the day. We're called as recruits in the army of light, and if we're missing from the battle, we know we just didn't count as much as we could have.

This is also why your big cause, when you find it and throw your weight behind it, will turn out to be even bigger than you hoped. This is why the hard work and the possible suffering are worth it. For whenever you are assisting in the reconciliation of all things to God, then you are part of The Biggest Cause of All.

STARTING OVER EVERY DAY

CHAPTER 11

LIVING BEYOND YOUR REGRETS

My brother, Jon, and I hope that by now you're feeling much better about your past, present, and future. We expect that your regret is no longer a source of pain like it used to be. We trust it has lost its power to hold you back from a better tomorrow. If God has already begun the process of redemption in your life, then you may even be looking upon your regret with fondness because being mindful about it has helped you escape from your Sorry Cycle and start over.

Way back at the beginning of this book, we told you this would happen. We could be confident about our promise because we know that our God is a Redeemer God. Always has been, always will be!

As this book draws to its close, we have one more promise to make to you, and it's the biggest one of all.

You can live beyond regrets *permanently.* The starting-over process is not just a one-time fix but rather a skill you can retain (like riding a bike) and employ whenever you need it. When something goes wrong in life—and of course that will continue to happen—you can recover your momentum quickly and keep moving forward. Living beyond regret can become a way of life.

The prophet Jeremiah was a man with big-time regrets. "I remember my affliction and my wandering, the bitterness and the gall," he said. And when he ruminated on those, he said, his soul was "downcast" within him.[1]

But he changed his focus from his Sorry Cycle to the promise of God's redemption. Suddenly the future looked like an endless progression of possibilities.

> Because of the LORD's great love we are not consumed,
>> for his compassions never fail.
> They are new every morning;
>> great is your faithfulness.[2]

New every morning.

God's mercies are served up fresh daily. So recovery is always a possibility. We can start over starting today . . . and starting again tomorrow . . . and starting the day after that too, if need be. Like a mighty river flowing from an inexhaustible source, God's redemption just keeps coming.

To show you how this can be, I want to tell you about the alternative to getting stuck in a Sorry Cycle. Bad things will continue to happen sometimes, but if you react well to them right away, you can get back on track without all the debilitating results of ruminating on your regrets. Instead, you can turn your experiences into a Starting Over Loop.

THE STARTING OVER LOOP

What are you going to do the next time something goes wrong and you feel regret? I hope you won't sink back into the old habit of dwelling on your regret pointlessly. Nor, I hope, will you try to hide from the regret. Your regret is an enemy you can turn into an ally. So develop the instinct of reacting to regret as quickly as possible by recognizing it, releasing it, and redeeming it. This way you only have to go around one time: a Starting Over Loop instead of a Sorry Cycle. One and done.

Sooner or later, you will have some kind of longing that fails to be fulfilled in a satisfying way. Okay. Take that as an opportunity to develop the instinct of responding *instantly* to regret by renewing your focus on God as the number one priority in your life. With that godly perspective, work on how you can fulfill your longing in a different way, one that is directed God-ward.

Supposedly Albert Einstein defined *insanity* as doing the same thing over and over again and expecting different results. When regret comes along, do the sane thing and make a change.

You can't speed up God's redemption—he'll act in his own time no matter what you do. But you can reduce the time you waste in feeling sorry for yourself. And you can reduce the time you spend in making futile responses to your regrettable situation. Rather than getting stuck in the Sorry Cycle, rotate through the Starting Over Loop a single time and then get on with life.

The Apollo 13 astronauts, dealing with life-threatening mechanical failures in their capsule and limited in rocket fuel, took advantage of something called *free return trajectory.* They looped around the moon and used its gravity to slingshot them back to earth. You can do the same with your regrets. You don't have to orbit them permanently, tethered to the gravity they exert. Instead, you can use their own force to propel yourself back onto a better course in life.

Yes, life will sometimes throw you for a loop. But you don't have to stay in a Sorry Cycle. Each time, you can turn it into a Starting Over Loop instead.

To help you in this, I want to make sure the starting-over process of the three Rs—recognize, release, redeem—is fixed firmly in your mind, because it's something you want to be clear about the moment you need it. Let me tell you about my friend Randy.

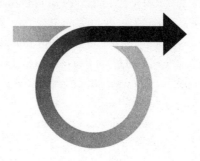

What the Heaven!?

On a Saturday night in October, thirty-four-year-old Randy was sitting in a friend's car trying to figure out how he had gotten to where he had in his life.[3] Here he was, a guy who had grown up in a loving home and then had gone on to become a junior-college All-American golfer, the captain of a Division 1 baseball team, and a professional golfer. Yet now he was broke, miserable, and all but friendless, living in his parents' home because he could no longer afford his own place. He admitted to himself that for many years he'd been a liar, a thief, and a manipulator. He ached inside every time he thought of the life he had taken when he'd been driving while drunk. The regrets weighing upon him were multiple and overwhelming.

Woven into most of his other sins and weaknesses was the problem of substance abuse. Randy had been an athlete who loved to win, but the truth was, after years of indulging, and then trying to stop indulging, drugs and alcohol had him defeated.

He had participated in Alcoholics Anonymous, and it had worked for him for a while. But one night he tried some "controlled drinking." For an alcoholic like him, though, controlled drinking was a fantasy. Of course he got drunk again. And of course the next day, when he woke up, his future seemed darker than ever. Sometimes the Sorry Cycle can close in on you.

That day, Randy called an old friend he hadn't seen in a while. Dustin used to be one of Randy's drinking buddies, but Randy knew Dustin had been sober for some time. Maybe he had the answer Randy was looking for.

"What should I do?" Randy asked, as they sat in Dustin's car in the driveway to Randy's parents' house.

Randy would have stood on his head and spun around ten times if that's what Dustin had told him to do. He was desperate to find a way out of his situation. But he wasn't prepared for what Dustin actually said.

"Go into your parents' house," Dustin counseled. "Say hello and goodnight to them. Then go into your room, hit your knees, and ask Jesus for help."

"What the hell?" exclaimed Randy.

But he did exactly what Dustin had told him to do. His prayer for help was a brief but heartfelt one. Then Randy crawled into bed and pulled the covers over him.

Here's what Randy said happened next.

"Something happened. It felt like nothing I had ever experienced. The feeling was warm, tingly, out of body. I don't know exactly how to describe it, but it lasted for a few minutes and when it was over I knew something supernatural had happened. I felt a peace come over me like never before."

The next morning Randy woke to the sound of the bedside phone ringing.

It was Dustin. Without even a hello, he said to Randy, "Would you like to go to church with me this morning?"

Randy hadn't been to church in a long time or even considered it. "What the hell?" he replied again to Dustin. But he agreed to go.

That morning the pastor said that if anybody confessed their sins to God and accepted Jesus as the One who gave up his life to forgive us, they could begin a new life with God. Up to this point, Randy had considered his sins to be unforgivable. The possibility of starting over seemed like a miraculous opportunity. Sobbing uncontrollably, he responded to the invitation and walked toward the front of the auditorium to accept God's forgiveness. He remembers, "These tears pouring out of my eyes were the release of all the guilt, shame, and remorse that I thought I would carry forever."

Twenty years have passed. Randy has still not gotten over what happened that day, and he hopes he never will. He says, "Today I have a beautiful wife and daughter. Today I have purpose and I am a pastor. Who would have thought?

"A gracious, merciful, loving God—that's who!"

MAKE YOUR MOVES

Let's use my friend Randy's story to review the three Rs. I want to merge them with the Sorry Cycle so that you can see the difference clearly between the repetitive Sorry Cycle and the one-and-done Starting Over Loop.

Randy's Sorry Cycle

I know a little about my friend Randy's motivations in his earlier years, so I can tell you that his drinking and many of his other problems stemmed from a misplaced longing for success. He saw himself first and foremost as an athlete, and he wanted to win. He also wanted all the rewards that come with being a winner.

For Randy, being a professional golfer was great. Yet somehow it didn't satisfy him. He didn't know that temporary success and fleeting rewards are always inadequate unless we seek our greatest satisfaction in God. If Randy had aligned his life purpose with The Biggest Cause of All, it would have made a huge difference. But he didn't. The affairs, the greed, the indulgence in mood-altering substances were all ways of trying to fulfill his longing in insufficient ways, and over time he started to feel the grinding of regret upon his spirit.

It was classic Sorry Cycle stuff. He had a longing. He tried to satisfy it with things that never could fulfill that longing. He felt regret about it. He had more longing. He doubled down on his misguided attempts . . . and so it went.

We all can relate to what it feels like to ride the sorry-go-round.

Randy's first move—to recognize his regret

When he woke up after his latest drunken episode and the world looked very dark and lonely, Randy clearly recognized his regret at having lost to the power of addictive substances. This particular regret was all balled up with other regrets he had about the mistakes of his past. Randy was a man of action, and his regrets were all regrets of action. *I wish I had never cheated on my wife. I wish I had never gotten behind the wheel after drinking. I wish hadn't been such a jerk and alienated my friends.* In fact, I'm sure that Randy could have articulated regrets in all of the major areas of spirituality, relationships, health, finances, and purpose. (Let's not point fingers. Most of us could do the same!) Randy realized that he didn't like himself drunk or sober.

What shows me that Randy wasn't merely ruminating on his regrets but rather was facing them constructively is that he was looking for what he could do differently. "What should I do?" he asked Dustin. That's the cry of a man ready for a change.

When you reach this point and you recognize your regret, you will face it head-on, identify it for what it is, making it out to be neither too big nor too small, and then interrogate it for what it can teach you. You're not indulging sorrowful feelings. You're gathering valuable feedback for the change that's coming.

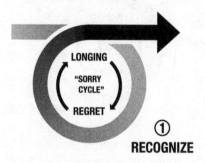

Randy's second move—to release his regret

Randy's regret release was about as dramatic as any I've ever seen. In his room, at the advice of Dustin, he prayed for Jesus's help—and God immediately gave him a sense of supernatural peace. Change was already under way! And the next day at church, after hearing the good news that forgiveness can be found in Jesus, the shame and guilt flooded out of him as the tears flooded out of his eyes.

If you are far from God, as Randy was, then turning your life over to Jesus for the first time is exactly what you need to do too. As Jon and I say in *Finding Your Way Back to God,* help has a name. His name is Jesus.

Turn to God, or turn back to him, through Jesus. And then you'll be able to release your regret. As needed . . .

- Ask forgiveness of others.
- Forgive others.
- Ask forgiveness of God.
- Forgive God and the world.
- Forgive yourself.

Holding on to a regret is just too great a burden. The weight will only grow over time. Whatever it takes, let it go.

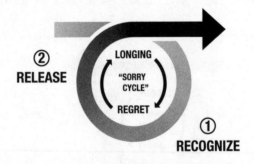

Randy's third move—to seek the redemption of his regret

All his life, Randy wanted to be a winner. But eventually he came up against a foe he couldn't defeat. And no, it wasn't drugs or alcohol. It was himself. He didn't know how to fulfill his legitimate longings in an adequate way. But when he surrendered to God, he became a winner.

Today, one-time athlete Randy is a pastor. He has also created a recovery ministry that merges the 12-Step recovery program with scriptural truth. It is helping many people find victory over their addictions.

God will redeem your regrets too. You need to trust him and wait expectantly for him to act. In the meantime, it makes sense to take whatever preparations you think God might wish to use in bringing about redemption. Just remember that God doesn't always act in the way we expect—he acts *beyond* our expectations!

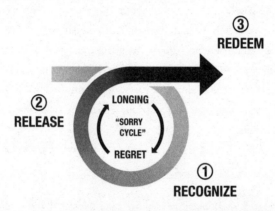

On the next couple of pages, I want to speak to you, particularly if you're feeling a little frustrated right now. Maybe you're thinking, *I get the three Rs. And I understand how they ought to work in a one-time Starting Over Loop— sounds good! But so far it's not working for me.*

Let's take a look at what you've been doing and see if we can find out what is going wrong.

TROUBLESHOOTING

If you're still having trouble getting past your regrets, run a diagnostic on the recognize-release-redeem protocol as you have been practicing it. Where in the process is the failure occurring? Somewhere a warning indicator is blinking.

Instead of recognizing your regret, are you turning a blind eye to it?

Starting over starts with admitting we have a regret and analyzing it for what it can teach us. Yet there can be a number of reasons why we may be reluctant to do this. For example, some people don't understand why recognizing a regret is important. Others might be too lazy or too discouraged to try it. But if you are balking right at the beginning of the process, most likely it's because you don't want to deal with the pain it will bring to the surface.

If you are afraid of regret pain, I can understand that. And it's true—at first, facing your regret *can* arouse suffering. It's touching a wound. Yet there is something about critically analyzing your regret that drains some of the suffering out of it. Recognizing your regret will put your regret in perspective. And eventually put it behind you.

So be willing to risk short-term pain for the long-term reward that will follow.

Instead of releasing your regret, are you holding on to it?

Our feelings about our regrets can sometimes get turned upside down and inside out until they don't bear any resemblance to reality. Maybe you're feeling sorry for yourself, or you blame yourself, and in some perverse way you don't want to give that up. Or you're so mad at God, the world, or some perceived enemy of yours that the anger has started to feel like a duty. You'd rather go on living with your regret than make a change.

You may have heard of the Stockholm syndrome, which is a psychological condition in which hostages have sympathy with or identify with their captors. Well, I've told you that you should love your regrets. But don't love them to the point where you want to remain in their captivity! Love your regrets as events from your past that can prove instructive for your future, not as present experiences you're willing to give control of your life.

Go ahead—be a party pooper at your own pity party. Relax your resistance to the voice of God inside your spirit that's telling you it's time to let go of the bad feelings.

Instead of redeeming **your regret, are you** resisting **redemption?**

To receive God's redemption of our regrets, we need to have a posture of openness to what he will bring. Instead, though, we can become closed off to his work. We're not looking to the future; we're still focused on our regret in the past. Instead of waiting expectantly for God to act, we're hardly giving him the time of day.

Is this your problem? If so, why?

I can think of a couple possibilities.

One is that you might have too little trust.

Maybe you don't really believe that God can or will redeem your regret. If that's the case, here's some advice for you:

First, recall God's promises.

Second, remember his might and what he's done over and over again, both in the lives of others and in your own life, to turn circumstances around.

Third, renew your faith in him.

In desperation, a father once asked Jesus to rescue his son, who was horribly afflicted by an evil spirit.[4]

Jesus replied, "Everything is possible for one who believes."

That must have sounded like music to the father's ears. Yet he wondered if he could really believe that help has the name of Jesus.

The father's response to Jesus is one that many of us can recognize as reflecting how we often feel: "I do believe; help me overcome my unbelief!"

If doubt about the possibility of redemption wars with faith inside you, pray for the faith to triumph.

Another problem might be anticipatory resistance: you aren't willing to accept whatever type of redemption God might bring. You don't know what

God has waiting for you behind curtain number one, but if it isn't the kind of redemption you want, you'd rather hold on to the regret you've already got. For example, you might be feeling that if you can't have a lost lover back, you don't want some other kind of relationship redemption. Or if you aren't healed of your illness, you don't want a different kind of health redemption. So your spirit is rebellious, even before you know what God is going to do.

In a way, this is a trust issue too. You're not doubting *whether* God can redeem. You're doubting that how he redeems your life will meet with your approval. It's like you're ready to regret your redemption. Now that's messed up!

Here's where you've got to believe that God sees much more of what's going on than you do and that he knows what's best. Any parent knows that kids don't always understand that our decisions are in their best interests. Even more so, God's decisions are in our best interests too.

Try a little humility.

Venture some receptivity.

In faith, tell God you'll welcome whatever redemption he brings.

HELPING OTHERS START OVER

The way that God redeems our regrets is never quite the same for any two people. Nevertheless, I believe there is one piece of redemption that every one of us can share in. I'm talking about passing on to others what we've learned about escaping regret. We can become partners to help our friends break out of their own Sorry Cycle and live beyond their own regrets. This is exactly what Randy did when he started a program to help others who are desperate for a way out of the bondage of addiction.

So, who do you know who is stuck in regret over something that happened in the past? If names come to your mind immediately, write them down before you forget them.

Some folks may not openly talk about their regrets, and yet they may give away clues that they are revolving in a Sorry Cycle. These clues can include the following:

- They are depressed.
- They verbally cut themselves down.
- They exhibit self-destructive behaviors.
- They are angry and bitter.
- They are discouraged or hopeless.
- They are not energized.
- They are not looking toward the future.
- The pattern of their life is better described as a *rut* than a *routine*.

These are people who need to start over. And you can help! Record the names of your friends and acquaintances who reveal their regrets by their behavior.

Wouldn't you have liked someone to step in when you were discouraged by your own Sorry Cycle? Do the same for someone else. Be a breakout partner, a redemption agent, a starting-over cheerleader.

First, practice telling your story of getting stuck in the Sorry Cycle of longing and regret and then eventually finding your way out. Consider this idea: approach it the way that an entrepreneur would convey a new business idea to a colleague—with a napkin drawing. On a paper napkin (or other piece of paper), draw the Sorry Cycle you got stuck in as well as the Starting Over Loop of recognition, release, and redemption that set you free. You can use the diagrams in this chapter as a guide. Narrate your story succinctly and clearly while you're completing the drawing.

Once you feel confident about sharing your own story with another person, your next step is to pray a prayer like this:

Redeemer God, thank you for the redemption that you have given to me. Help me now to be an agent of redemption in someone else's life. Direct me to someone I could share my story of starting over with. Help me to find the right time and the right way to help this person begin the process of starting over. Amen.

Because God loves to change hurting lives, he loves this kind of prayer—and he'll answer it too! So just as you waited on the edge of your seat for him to send redemption to you, now wait with your eyes open and a sense of expectancy in your heart for him to nudge you toward someone else who needs to take the first step toward freedom from regret. You may wish to pick up an extra copy of this book to give to that person, or be willing to share your own copy.

Somebody else is going to have a life-changing *Aha!* moment when you sketch your drawing from memory and tell your story. Great entrepreneurial ideas are often described as "disruptive" because of how they alter the status quo of business. Likewise, the vision of starting over that you give to a person stuck in a Sorry Cycle will be disruptive for him or her . . . in the best possible sense.

In a beautiful way that reminds me so much of how God works, the completion of your own Starting Over Loop can become the beginning of someone else's.

DEAN AND THE DIVINE

I have a friend named Dean who works with college students at Michigan State University. Every morning Dean prays for what he calls "divine appointments," that is, he asks God to direct him to people during the day whom he can bless. And then he goes through his day assuming that whoever he talks to might be a divine appointment.

One time he had a canceled appointment, and instead of checking e-mail or getting on Facebook, he decided to pray. *God, how do you want me to use this time?* He sat still, in a spiritually receptive frame of mind, and the name of a student—Janice—came to him. Dean knew Janice was far from God, and he sensed that he was supposed to explain to her how she could find her way back to God through Jesus. So he called her and asked to meet for coffee.

When they sat down, he said, "Janice, I was praying and your name came to mind. I felt like I was supposed to share with you how you can find your way back to God."

She started crying.

Dean immediately recoiled. He said, "Oh, I'm sorry. I shouldn't have just blurted that out. I'm not being very sensitive."

Then Janice interrupted, "No. That's not it. I just can't believe that you are here. Last night I was talking to some girls in my dorm. As it got later, the conversation grew deeper and I shared with them some of the mistakes I had made my first year away from home. They then started talking about what it means to find forgiveness in Jesus. At first I sort of blew it off, but after I returned to my room, I couldn't stop thinking about it. All night I couldn't sleep. I didn't know what to do. So I tried praying this morning, asking God if he would bring someone to me today to tell me how to get this forgiveness." She smiled and said, "And here you are. I just can't believe it!"

I love talking to Dean because every day of his life is a mini-adventure. He never has a day that is the same old same old.

Why don't you try living in a spiritually adventurous way like Dean? Dare to pray for God to send you across the path of someone who needs to start over. When God puts you together with someone in need, listen with empathy to this person's story. Then reach for the nearest napkin.

FOREVER NEW

After everything we have been through together in the course of this book, I have one last truth I want to set in your heart. I want to tell you where the Starting Over Loop is headed—your final destination.

Through a process of starting over, we can put our regrets behind us in this life. Although our regrets don't disappear, they do recede. They lose their power over us, shrinking to a point where they no longer pose obstacles to forward motion. That's an amazing thing. But how awesome it would be if those regrets could be erased entirely—and that's just what's going to happen one day!

For those of us who have found our way back to God, we've got a new existence coming. It's an eternal life that knows no regret.

Listen to these words from one who was granted a vision of what's in store:

I heard a loud voice from the throne saying, "Look! God's dwelling place is now among the people, and he will dwell with them. They will be his people, and God himself will be with them and be their God. 'He will wipe every tear from their eyes. There will be no more death' or mourning or crying or pain, for the old order of things has passed away."

He who was seated on the throne said, "I am making everything new!"[5]

In this new, eternal existence, we will have no more regret from the past or possibility of regret in the future. The pain, the tears, the grief will all be wiped away, never to return.

Regrets of action—gone! We won't hurt anybody, ever.

Regrets of inaction—gone! We won't ever miss out.

Regrets of reaction—also gone! The new heavens and the new earth will be a totally safe place for all of us—nobody will ever hurt us.

Regret is barred from heaven. No bondage there; only freedom. No sorrow; only joy. There, we won't have to hope or strive for a new beginning, because we will live in newness all the time.

And so, if you are weighed down with regret, Jon and I urge you, don't wait! Start over starting today. What you'll get will be nothing less than a foretaste of the everlasting joy to come.

CHAPTER 12

HOW TO HELP OTHERS START OVER

I don't know him."

"I was not with him."

"I don't know him or what you are talking about!"[1]

These words must have haunted Peter for a long time. His repeated denials of Jesus were no doubt the most regrettable moments of his life. I have to believe that every day and perhaps several times a day he was overwhelmed by this regret of action.

Before you write off Peter, you should ask yourself how you would have responded in a similar situation. If your life were on the line and someone asked you about your relationship with an accused criminal, what would you have said? Most of us, if we're honest with ourselves, would've responded similarly to Peter. Driven by fear, doubt, and self-preservation, we would find it hard to act otherwise. Especially when we remember that we have the opportunity to speculate with the end of the story in mind. Peter was living in the moment, facing the unknown, with no knowledge of the Resurrection.

This raises a question: If you had fallen as Peter did, who would you turn to for help at a second chance or for an opportunity to start over? Where would you look for a way forward after a most regrettable evening?

Let me pose one more question. Put the shoe on the other foot—if Peter were your friend and he came to you stuck in regret and the Sorry Cycle, how would you respond?

The patterns that we've set out in this book to help you find a life beyond regret also apply to helping a friend, family member, or loved one start over! Once you take the following steps to start fresh, you have the opportunity to help others begin the path to new life. It's as simple as *recognize, release,* and *redeem.* Knowing that, how would you help a friend start over?

Two Decades of Regret

My friend Matthew was haunted by the same regret every day for two decades. Sitting across from me over breakfast at one of our favorite diners, he looked at me with tears in his eyes and said, "For twenty years I have felt like I had the burden of not just living one life but of living two."

Matthew and I became friends because our sons ran on the same high school cross-country team and we loved the sport. I knew him as a self-made man. He overcame an abusive home life as a child by moving out on his own as a teenager. He went on to become a successful college athlete, marry a beautiful woman, start his own company, and enjoy all the benefits of success.

We were both gasping for breath, trying to keep up with our boys during a cross-country meet, when he said to me, "Hey, I'd like for us to talk sometime; I've got some stuff I'm trying to work out." Now we were having breakfast together, and he was sharing with me a story he had told only his wife. With obvious emotion, he began to unburden his soul of a regret he had carried for years and years.

"When I was in grad school out in California, my best friend was a guy named Josh. He was a really good guy. The kind of guy I always aspired to be. I was the best man in his wedding, and since I was newly engaged, I wanted him to be the best man in my wedding."

Matthew paused to compose himself. He took a sip of coffee and a bite of toast and continued.

"Dave, it was exactly twenty years ago today that we were in a car accident. I survived. Josh did not. I watched him die in that car crash. It was all my fault.

His parents refused to speak to me and held me responsible for his death. They wanted nothing to do with me. Every day since, I have lived with the guilt and shame of that moment. I decided to never tell anyone. So for twenty years I have felt like I had the burden of not just living one life but of living two lives: my own and Josh's, in a futile effort to somehow make up for his loss."

Matthew's story was one of the saddest stories I've ever heard. Like Peter, he felt a relentless burden from causing tremendous pain and loss to those he loved dearly. But let's push pause on his story and go back to the challenge we issued in the previous chapter to help others start over. There are people like Matthew and Peter all around you. In the same way you have regrets, so do the people in your family, your neighbors next door, the people you work with, and the friends you hang out with. We all have regrets. We all have stuff that plagues us from the past.

If we believe it's true that God's mercies never come to an end—"they are new every morning" (Lamentations 3:23)—how do we help others come to that same belief? How do we help others start over just as we have been able to start over?

Let me tell you the rest of Matthew's story and highlight three lessons to help others start over.

Lesson 1: Prayer Helps Others Recognize Regret

I began Matthew's story with us together in a local diner. What I didn't tell you was that for two and a half years before that day, I had been regularly praying for Matthew. In a letter Peter wrote to Christ-followers, we find encouragement to pray for one another: "The eyes of the Lord are on the righteous, and his ears are open to their prayer" (1 Peter 3:12).

Almost daily in my journal I would write five to ten names, including Matthew's, asking God for an opportunity to help them start over. I believe God's Spirit moved in Matthew partially in response to my prayers. The opportunity finally came when Matthew said, "Hey, I'd like for us to talk sometime; I've got some stuff I'm trying to work out." God's Spirit was working in my friend to help him *recognize* he was stuck in his regret. Don't you want that for the people God has put in your life?

Starting Over Prayer List

Who are five people that you will begin praying for? I gave you some clues in chapter 11 for how to identify people stuck in the Sorry Cycle. I even gave you a prayer to pray. Now I want you to make a list of people for whom you will begin to pray:

1. _____
2. _____
3. _____
4. _____
5. _____

Lesson 2: *Friends Help Others* Release *Regret*

Matthew began by recognizing his regrets and sharing those with me over breakfast, but I knew we needed to work together to help him move further through the Starting Over Loop. He needed the times of refreshing that come with repentance and forgiveness. And what he needed next was to experience the release of his regrets.

After our breakfast conversation, I felt as though the forgiveness that Matthew needed would come when he discovered he was not alone in dealing with his regrets. So, I invited him to my small group that just so happened to be discussing how to start over. When he agreed to come with his wife, I knew it would be a good experience for him, but I had no idea how good.

The first night we were supposed to meet, several people had last-minute scheduling conflicts and were not able to join us . It ended up being just six of us gathered in our living room: my wife, Sue, and me; Matthew and his wife; and

Brent and Kelly King. You'll remember we told the Kings' story in chapter 5 about starting over after the tragic murder of their daughter. It was an unusually small group that night, and while pastors rarely like to see a decline in attendance of any kind, God knew exactly what he was doing with it being only the six of us.

About fifteen minutes into our discussion, the Kings began to share their story of having to start over after losing Chelsea, their beautiful seventeen-year-old daughter. As they spoke about forgiveness and redemption in the midst of the most regrettable situation, we could feel God transforming our living room into a holy place. The Spirit of God was clearly present.

The Kings finished their story and then Matthew spoke. "First, I'm so sorry," he said to the Kings. "I didn't know . . ." Then he continued, "The two of you are so brave . . ." Hearing someone share a story of regret that was so painful actually gave him the courage to share his own. He began to talk about that day twenty years ago, the accident, his friend's death, and the burden of trying to live two lives. For the second time in two weeks he was sharing his story out loud with someone other than his wife. Both times he was reminded that our God is a forgiving God. Matthew was discovering the release and refreshment of forgiveness.

A couple of days later Matthew called me and explained that he had shared his story with several other people we both knew. He said, "Dave, every time I share my story it's like my burden gets lighter and lighter!" It reminded me of these words from Peter: "Humble yourselves, therefore, under God's mighty hand, that he may lift you up in due time" (1 Peter 5:6). That's what was happening to Matthew. He was humbling himself before God and others. And in turn, God was lifting him up. Then Matthew said to me, "Hey, Dave, since my birthday is on Easter, and I feel like I'm starting over with a new life, I want to be baptized!"

On Easter morning Matthew shared his story with the whole church family:

I did not have a relationship with God. I did not think about it. Having a relationship with God was not a goal or objective of mine. My mentality has always been that if you want to get something done, you can only rely on yourself! And that is how I approached the world for many years.

Josh was my roommate in graduate school. So in February Josh and I went to a concert and we were in a car wreck. Josh died in that car wreck. I was extremely emotionally devastated by the loss of my friend. I felt very responsible and I was very angry with God.

So I decided then that I would live two lives—one for me and one for my friend Josh. I began trying to do that in everything I did. And consequently everything I tried to achieve was never enough. It never made me feel differently. I still felt angry. I felt very alone. It didn't matter how hard I tried or what I accomplished, something was still missing. I just kept walking through life carrying what felt like a bag of bricks. I never considered that I could put them down or ask for help.

Then I got invited to go to a small group. I didn't really know what that was because I'd never been in a small group. I was very nervous. And I was nervous because the group was about regret. I remember thinking, *How appropriate that my first small group is about the very subject I need to learn the most about.* That group really opened my eyes.

The tipping point for me was on the twentieth anniversary of this car accident that killed my friend. It had been a very dark day, a very upsetting day. All the people around me had no idea why I was so upset. It was on that day I shared my story. And what I found was that as I started sharing my story with my family and close friends, every time I talked about my regrets it was like I was taking a brick out of my bag and putting it down and my load was getting lighter and lighter and lighter.

For most of my life I thought that asking for help was a sign of weakness. What I have come to realize is that asking for help is a sign of strength. If you really want some help, the best place you can go is to ask God for help and accept Jesus into your life.

Then, surrounded by family and friends he had invited from across the country, along with his new small group, Matthew was baptized. It had been a long journey through the Starting Over Loop, but my friend Matthew was being released from his regrets.

Starting Over Small Group

Who from your "Starting Over Prayer List" could you invite to join you and read this book together?

What if you began a Starting Over small group? There is no greater universal need than the need to start over and live beyond your regrets. We all have friends, family, neighbors, and coworkers who need to start over. When people come together and authentically discuss starting over, it creates an environment that frees people to be released from their regrets.

Lesson 3: God's Truth Helps Others Redeem Regret

I'm tempted to tell you that after Matthew was baptized he never looked back and continuously lived a life beyond his regrets! But that wouldn't be true. For several weeks he lived with an everyday conscious awareness of God's grace and forgiveness that allowed him to not regret his regrets. But within a few months he began to struggle.

Disappointed?

You shouldn't be. Isn't that how it goes for all of us? It certainly is for me! For a season I will live with an everyday awareness that God loves me no matter what and that he has a dream for my life. But then I struggle. And I forget. So did Matthew. We all do.

So what do we do when we have friends and people we love who know their regrets and know they are forgiven but still struggle with their past? We should do what Jesus did with Peter—remind them of God's truth in their life.

PETER AND JESUS—PART 2

I want us to dig a little deeper into the story we told about Peter in chapter 2. We pick up the story just after Peter had denied Jesus three times. And now he is about to have his first personal conversation with Jesus since those denials. At this point, it's hard to imagine he wasn't sinking deep into the Sorry Cycle of regret.

As he approaches Jesus, a familiar aroma fills the air. Jesus is there, cooking breakfast over a charcoal fire.

Smells have a way of conjuring up memories, don't they? The aroma of hot, buttered crescent rolls tells me it's Thanksgiving dinner at my mom and dad's. Just a whiff of pumpkin chocolate chip cookies says it's fall and my wife is making my kids' favorite treats. The stench of rotting produce reminds me that my wife is about to tell me to take out the garbage! Smells bring to mind memories and, with them, corresponding emotions.

What I recently discovered is that there are two charcoal fires mentioned in the Gospels, and Peter was at both of them. It was at the first charcoal fire when he said, "I don't know." Then again, "I don't know him." And finally a third time, "I do not know this man!"

So now he is around the second charcoal fire, and as the smell of his betrayal fills the air, Jesus serves Peter breakfast. It's time to break the silence:

Jesus said to Simon Peter, "Simon son of John, do you love me more than these?"

"Yes, Lord," he said, "you know that I love you."

Jesus said, "Feed my lambs."[2]

We already mentioned that this question, asked three times, corresponds perfectly to Peter's three regrettable denials. But there is another layer I hope you get out of this interaction, as it pertains to your friends. Jesus gives us a prime example in his exchange with Peter. He helps his friend begin to realize the truth so that he can begin to start over!

Redemptive Truth: You Are Loved by God

First, Jesus confirms his relationship and his love for Peter. Implied in Jesus's question *"Do you love me?"* is a priceless reassurance: *"Because I still love you."* Anyone who dares ask the question "Do you love me?" has usually in that moment confessed his love for the person he is asking. It would be cruel to ask someone "Do you love me?" if you didn't have a genuine love for the person you are asking. Jesus's question to Peter, "Do you love me?" came from a place of deep and passionate love for him.

When we know we are loved, we can find the courage to face our regrets. For the first time, second time, third time, and even the seventy-seventh time! Jesus doesn't chastise Peter. He doesn't rehash what happened. Nor does he blow it off as no big deal. He conveys the truth about his love for Peter and gives Peter the opportunity to affirm his love back. He is reassuring Peter of this truth: I love you!

Redemptive Truth: You Have a Purpose from God.

But Jesus does something else too: Jesus confirms that Peter has a clear purpose given to him by God. After each affirmation of love comes this charge: *"Feed my sheep."*

Jesus, who earlier refers to himself as "the Good Shepherd," commissions Peter to join him in carrying out his mission. By giving Peter a job to do he is saying, *"Peter, you still have a purpose to fulfill. You are not disqualified. I'm not done with you. I need you. I want you to lead and care for my followers."* After accepting the truth that they are loved by God, your friends who are struggling with regrets need to be reminded that God is not finished with them and has a purpose for them.

This scene between Jesus and Peter is one of the most spectacular exchanges in the entire Bible. Jesus refuses to let Peter get stuck in the Sorry Cycle or mired in his regrets. He confirms the truth that Peter is loved by God, and he confirms the truth that Peter has a purpose from God. That is what empowers Peter to move on from his regret and start over.

Share the Truth of Love and Purpose

This is what your friends need to understand today: What Jesus did for Peter, he wants to do for them and the people they love! If you or someone you know is still stuck in regret, God is saying to all of us today:

> "I love you with no strings attached. Nothing will ever change how I feel about you."

> "No matter what you've done or not done or how you have or have not responded to your regret up till now, it is never too late to begin again."

> "You are not damaged goods. You can start over, and I have a plan and purpose for your life."

What Jesus did for Peter, he wants to do for you too. He wants to confirm your relationship. He wants to confirm your purpose. Not only that, he wants to do this for the people around you, and he wants to do it through you. He wants to be in relationship with them. He has not given up on them, and he has a purpose for their life!

My Friend Was Starting Over . . . Again

Four months after Matthew's baptism, we sat down for lunch, and he confessed to me that while his commitment to Jesus was real and his conviction that he was forgiven wasn't shaken, he was still struggling. I told him, "Welcome to the team. We all struggle." Over lunch I began to explain some of the same redemptive truths that Jesus shared with Peter: that God and I love him and that he has a purpose! With those new truths, Matthew began to establish some new disciplines that would keep him going back to the truth source of Scripture. He also began to discover ways he could share his newfound faith with teens who had gone through some of the same tough stuff he went through. He was starting over again and helping others start over at the same time.

It's a two-part message we are commissioned to give to others, even those facing what seems like insurmountable regret. It's a simple but life-changing message: (1) You are loved, and (2) God has a purpose for your life.

Truths for Starting Over

"Godly sorrow brings repentance that leads to salvation and leaves no regret, but worldly sorrow brings death" (2 Corinthians 7:10).

"And we know that in all things God works for the good of those who love him, who have been called according to his purpose" (Romans 8:28).

"Because of the LORD's great love we are not consumed, for his compassions never fail. They are new every morning; great is your faithfulness" (Lamentations 3:22–23).

"If we confess our sins, he is faithful and just and will forgive us our sins and purify us from all unrighteousness" (1 John 1:9).

"Therefore, if anyone is in Christ, the new creation has come: The old has gone, the new is here!" (2 Corinthians 5:17).

"As far as the east is from the west, so far has he removed our transgressions from us" (Psalm 103:12).

You Can Do It!

This truth, that you can live beyond regret, is too good to keep to yourself. Share it with a friend, a family member, someone at work, or a person God leads you to. These are three simple ways you can help anyone start over:

- You can pray.
- You can be a friend.
- You can share God's truth.

Living Beyond Regrets Work Sheet

Step 1. Recognize Your Regret

What is your regret?

_____

_____

Is it a . . .

[ ] Regret of action (You did something you now wish you hadn't done.)

[ ] Regret of inaction (You failed to do something you now wish you had done.)

[ ] Regret of reaction (Something happened to you, and you now wish you hadn't responded to it like you did.)

Who was involved?

_____

What happened?

_____

When did it happen?

_____

Where did it happen?

_____

Why did it happen?

_____

How did it happen?

_____

How has this regret affected you mentally, spiritually, and emotionally?

_____

_____

What does this regret teach you about what you need to do more of, do less of, or do differently in the future?

_____

_____

Step 2. Release Your Regret

In the situation that you regret, did you commit a sin?

[ ] Yes

[ ] No

If yes, what was it?

_____

_____

Action steps:

- Ask forgiveness of God.
- Forgive yourself.

Did you make a mistake (not a sinful one)?

[ ] Yes

[ ] No

If yes, what was the mistake?

_____

_____

Action step:
- Forgive yourself.

Did you hurt someone else?
[ ] Yes
[ ] No
If yes, who did you hurt and how did you hurt this person?

_____

_____

_____

Action steps:
- If possible, ask forgiveness of the other person and seek to make amends or reconcile.
- Forgive yourself.

Did someone else hurt you?
[ ] Yes
[ ] No
If yes, who hurt you and how did this person hurt you?

_____

_____

_____

Action steps:
- Resist the temptation to blame God or yourself.
- Forgive the offender.

Did impersonal life circumstances hurt you?

[ ] Yes

[ ] No

If yes, what hurt you and how did it hurt you?

_____

_____

Action steps:

- Forgive the fallen world that exposed you to this dangerous circumstance.
- Resist the temptation to blame God; instead turn to him for comfort and restoration.

Step 3. Redeem Your Regret

What kind of redemption of your regret are you hoping for?

_____

_____

Write out a prayer, asking God to redeem your regret and telling him that you trust him to bring something beautiful out of the ugliness of your regret.

_____

_____

_____

_____

Keeping in mind that you don't necessarily know what kind of redemption God has in store for your regret, what steps can you take to prepare for what you *think* he will do?

_____

_____

GROUP STUDY GUIDE

CHAPTER 1. THE SORRY CYCLE

Breaking the Ice

Was there ever a time you simply wanted a do-over? Maybe it was an embarrassing moment or an incident that lives on in infamy among your family or friends. If you feel comfortable, share this story or incident with the group.

Digging Deeper

Regret is a powerful word. When you hear the word *regret,* what comes to mind?

How have you found yourself or someone you love stuck in the Sorry Cycle of longing and regret?

In chapter 1, the authors describe three kinds of regrets: regrets of action, inaction, and reaction. Which bucket do you think would hold the majority of people's regrets? Which bucket would hold the majority of your regrets?

In what area of life do you think people experience the greatest regrets?

How could our longing for God be linked to our deepest regrets?

In Ecclesiastes 3:11, we read that God "has also set eternity in the human heart." Isaiah the prophet wrote, "My soul yearns for you in the night; in the morning my spirit longs for you" (26:9). How could our attempts to fulfill our longing for God and eternity lead to regret?

Bringing It Home

How can we create a safe place where we are comfortable talking about our deepest regrets?

Take twenty to thirty minutes of quiet time to reflect on any regrets you may be holding on to that leave you stuck in the Sorry Cycle. As you reflect, identify them as regrets of action, inaction, or reaction. After you place your regrets in buckets, ask God to help you trust him to help you escape the Sorry Cycle.

CHAPTER 2. LOVE YOUR REGRETS

Breaking the Ice

What is your favorite memory or story of a time you spent around a campfire?

Digging Deeper

Read Luke 22:54–62, the story of Peter's denials of Jesus.

Peter denied Jesus and immediately regretted his decision. In what bucket would you place Peter's regret: action, inaction, or reaction? What about his regret makes you place it in that bucket?

Peter acted as a spokesperson and leader of Jesus's disciples, but he disowned

Jesus when his life was in danger. What do you suppose he was thinking as the reality of his denial set in?

Read John 21:15–19.

How do you think Peter felt as he had this conversation with Jesus? Do you think his feelings changed as Jesus repeatedly asked him, "Do you love me?"

Peter went on to be a great leader in the church and remained faithful to the calling he had heard from Jesus during that breakfast around a fire. How do you suppose Peter remembered that breakfast later on in his life?

The title of chapter 2 is "Love Your Regrets." What do you think makes it possible for us to love our regrets?

Bringing It Home
In what ways have your own regrets offered important and helpful feedback?

Think about the regrets you continually replay in your head. How might you, like Peter, begin to learn from your regrets and move beyond them?

Chapter 3. Step #1: Recognize Your Regrets

Breaking the Ice
Have you ever gone through a whole day or a party with something glaringly wrong about your outfit or appearance, but no one said anything? Would anyone like to share that story with the group?

Digging Deeper
Why is it so difficult to face our regrets head-on? What would you say is the most common way people avoid dealing with their regrets?

In chapter 3, we read about the aftermath of King David's most regretful affair with Bathsheba, when he was confronted by his friend Nathan. How do you think David was feeling when Nathan approached him? How do you think Nathan was feeling?

How would you say David was hiding his regret? Was it denial? distraction? suppression?

Just moments after Nathan confronted him, David recognized his regret and said, "I have sinned against the LORD" (2 Samuel 12:13). What is significant about David confessing his sin to Nathan? Why did David say he had "sinned against the LORD"?

Bringing It Home

If someone were to confront you about the regrets you've hidden away, how would you react?

Do you have someone who can act as a Nathan in your life? How might you give permission to one of your close friends to speak into your regrets as Nathan spoke to David?

Take a moment to reflect on these questions: What regret have you yet to confront head-on? What would it look like for you to fully recognize this regret?

CHAPTER 4. STEP #2: RELEASE YOUR REGRETS

Breaking the Ice

If you could take a time machine into the past to warn a historical character before he or she made a regretful decision, whom would you pick? Why did you choose that particular person?

Digging Deeper

Why do we have a tendency to hold on to regret?

Read Psalm 51. King David wrote this psalm after he was confronted about his affair with Bathsheba and confessed to his friend Nathan.

What words and phrases stand out to you most in Psalm 51? What about those words or phrases caught your attention?

In what ways do you see David recognizing and releasing his regret in this song?

Can you relate to David? How has God helped you release a regret and come out on the other side closer to him?

The process of letting go of our regrets is usually tied to forgiveness. Is it harder for you to receive forgiveness from others, extend it to others, or forgive yourself? How would you let go of a regret that may be the result of a life circumstance?

Lewis Smedes wrote that when we forgive, "We set a prisoner free and discover that the prisoner we set free is us." In what ways can forgiving someone else set you free from regret?

Bringing It Home

How could the five "Questions for Starting Over" in this chapter help you begin the process of releasing your regrets?

God wants you to be free. God gave us his Son, Jesus, so all of us might experience forgiveness and freedom. What do you need to let go of to truly be free?

CHAPTER 5. STEP #3: REDEEM YOUR REGRETS

Breaking the Ice

What is one food you hated as a child but have grown to like as an adult?

Digging Deeper

Redemption is what happens when unexpected good comes out of a situation that you could only expect to result in something bad. When have you seen unexpected good come from a situation when you could only have expected something bad?

In the New Testament, one of the words translated as "redemption" is the Greek word *lytrosis*. It was frequently used to mean redeem, liberate, ransom, or set free. Read the following scriptures where this word is found: Mark 10:45, Titus 2:14, and 1 Timothy 2:5–6. How would you summarize what these verses are saying about redemption?

How do these verses speak to the truth that Jesus wants to redeem us, even our regrets?

In Titus 2:14, we read that Jesus gave himself up for us so we would be purified, eager to do what is good. How might holding on to our regrets keep us from being eager to do what is good?

Why are we tempted to believe that some regrets are beyond God's power to redeem?

Bringing It Home

Romans 8:28 says, "And we know that in all things God works for the good of those who love him, who have been called according to his purpose." Think about what you have written off as irredeemable in your own life. What would it take for you to begin to see it through the eyes of Romans 8:28?

The first two steps in starting over are recognizing and releasing our regrets. The third step, redeeming our regrets, is different from the other two because it is something only God can do. How can we help each other begin to see how God may be redeeming our regrets?

Chapter 6. Finding Your Way Back

Breaking the Ice

What is one wild or rebellious act you committed as a teen or young adult that you now realize was foolish? (It doesn't have to be anything too embarrassing!)

Digging Deeper

When in your life do you most wish your thoughts would have turned toward God more? If you had thought about God during that time, how might that have impacted your circumstances?

Read the parable of the prodigal son from Luke 15:11–32.

Why did the son in this story choose to leave home? What was he longing for?

What led to the young man's regret in this story?

Why was he so reluctant to go home for help?

How did the father in the story respond when he recognized the young man's regret and his desire to be released from it by returning home to seek forgiveness from his father?

What is most compelling to you about this story? How does this story help us better understand how we can learn to live beyond our regrets?

Bringing It Home

Which of the following steps do you think are most important for you in letting go of your regrets regarding God?

- Ask forgiveness of others.
- Forgive others.
- Ask forgiveness of God.
- Forgive God and the world.
- Forgive yourself.

If you are ready to let God redeem any regrets you may have that are keeping you distant from him, consider praying this prayer: *Redeemer God, I want to believe in you. I want to know you. I want to be close to you. So if you are real, make yourself real to me. Awaken in me the ability to see that you are what's missing in my life. Show me Jesus. Amen.*

CHAPTER 7. HEARTS AT RISK

Breaking the Ice

If you feel comfortable sharing with the group, tell us about an embarrassing moment you had while on a date.

Digging Deeper

The authors write, "Researchers at two Illinois universities carried out a survey asking respondents to describe one memorable regret. A total of 47 percent of those regrets centered around relationships." Why do you think so many of our regrets have to do with relationships?

In which of the three buckets of regret do you think our relational regrets tend to fall: regrets of action, inaction, or reaction? What about these regrets makes you place them in that bucket?

Read the section "Putting the *Dys*– in *Dysfunction*." What is your reaction to this brief overview of the relational, familial history of the biblical patriarchs: Abraham, Isaac, and Jacob?

How can the relational history of these patriarchs give you hope?

How might you be stuck in the Sorry Cycle of longing and regret when it comes to some of your most significant relationships?

The apostle Paul wrote, "Be kind and compassionate to one another, forgiving each other, just as in Christ God forgave you" (Ephesians 4:32). How do these words and the example of Jesus motivate you to start over when it comes to your relational regrets?

Bringing It Home

Which of the following steps do you think are most important for you in letting go of your relational regrets?
- Ask forgiveness of others.
- Forgive others.
- Ask forgiveness of God.
- Forgive God and the world.
- Forgive yourself.

Think about one of your relational regrets. What is one way you can begin to escape the Sorry Cycle this week and move toward the three steps of recognizing, releasing, and redeeming that relational regret?

CHAPTER 8. FIT AS CAN BE

Breaking the Ice

What do you think are some of the most ridiculous health crazes ever (e.g., Thigh Master, Fruit Cleanse, Taco Cleanse—yes, it was a thing!)?

Digging Deeper

What percentage of people do you think would resonate or agree with this statement: "I wish I had taken better care of myself"? Why is that such a universal feeling?

Look at the word cloud at the start of chapter 8. Which of those words or phrases best reflects your regrets regarding your health or physical being?

Why do you think our culture is so obsessed with physical appearance? What are the damaging effects of this obsession? How does this lead to regret?

On the one hand Scripture says, "The LORD does not look at the things people look at. People look at the outward appearance, but the LORD looks at the heart" (1 Samuel 16:7). Yet on the other hand, Paul wrote in 1 Corinthians 6:19–20, "Do you not know that your bodies are temples of the Holy Spirit, who is in you, whom you have received from God? You are not your own; you were bought at a price. Therefore honor God with your bodies."

Based on these scriptures, how would you express, in your own words, what God wants for our physical bodies? How does that understanding help us move beyond any regrets we may have in regard to our physical health?

Bringing It Home

Which of the following steps do you think are most important for you in letting go of your physical regrets?

- Ask forgiveness of others.
- Forgive others.
- Ask forgiveness of God.
- Forgive God and the world.
- Forgive yourself.

Review the list of basic and perennial health advice under "Never Too Early, Never Too Late." Choose one item from the list that you can commit to working on this week.

CHAPTER 9. DOLLARS AND SENSE

Breaking the Ice

What was one of the worst investments or purchases you ever made? (Feel free to loosely describe it—no need to mention dollars here!)

Digging Deeper

Role-play or read out loud the "Bags of Gold" skit. You will need a volunteer for each of the four characters: Master, Servant 1, Servant 2, and Servant 3. The scenes are based on a parable Jesus told in Matthew 25:14–30.

In which of the three buckets of regret do you think most people's financial regrets tend to fall: regrets of action, inaction, or reaction? Why do you feel that they fall into that bucket?

When you have finished reading or acting out the scenes, read the truths from the parable listed under the "Disclaimer" subhead.

- Which of these truths is most applicable to your financial regret?
- Which of these truths is most important for you as you look to your finances in the future?

Why is it so difficult for people to talk about financial regrets?

Under "The Dumb Stuff" subhead, the authors reference Brad Klontz, an expert in financial psychology, who has identified four money scripts, or unconscious belief systems that affect how people approach money. Which of those scripts resonates most with you?

Bringing It Home

Which of the following steps do you think are most important for you in letting go of your financial regrets?

- Ask forgiveness of others.
- Forgive others.
- Ask forgiveness of God.
- Forgive God and the world.
- Forgive yourself.

In Malachi 3:10, God says to test him when it comes to our finances. Be generous toward him and see if he doesn't bless you abundantly. What would it look like for you to test God in this way? How might that help you escape the Sorry Cycle when it comes to your finances?

CHAPTER 10. MY WHY

Breaking the Ice

Whom have you always admired for giving his or her life to a great cause? What do you think was this person's motivation?

Digging Deeper

What are the most significant barriers that keep so many people from giving their lives to a bigger purpose? What keeps you from more fully giving your life to a bigger purpose?

How does the retelling of Moses's story under the "Just a Shepherd" subhead remind you that it's never too late to escape the Sorry Cycle of regret when it comes to your purpose in life?

What insights or assurances do you glean from the following scriptures as you consider how to start over and move toward giving your life to a great cause?

- "For we are God's handiwork, created in Christ Jesus to do good works, which God prepared in advance for us to do" (Ephesians 2:10).
- "For it is God who works in you to will and to act in order to fulfill his good purpose" (Philippians 2:13).
- "Now to him who is able to do immeasurably more than all we ask or imagine, according to his power that is at work within us . . ." (Ephesians 3:20).

What is a big cause that you might like to give more of your life to?

Bringing It Home

Which of the following steps do you think are most important for you in letting go of your purpose regrets?

- Ask forgiveness of others.
- Forgive others.
- Ask forgiveness of God.
- Forgive God and the world.
- Forgive yourself.

Which of these ideas (under "Missional Me" subhead) could you start working on this week in order to lay the groundwork for a future of greater significance?

- Evaluate your personal wiring.
- Reorganize your life, if necessary, to free up time and other resources.
- Start small.
- Be willing to make changes.
- Seek confirmation.

Chapter 11. Living Beyond Your Regrets

Breaking the Ice

Some research suggests that it takes ten thousand hours of practice in order to master a skill. What is something you have practiced over and over again in an effort to master it?

Digging Deeper

The prophet Jeremiah was a man with big-time regrets. He wrote, "I remember my affliction and my wandering, the bitterness and the gall. I well remember them, and my soul is downcast within me" (Lamentations 3:19–20).

Do you relate to Jeremiah's feelings of regret? If so, how?

But he changed his focus from a Sorry Cycle of regret to the promise of God's redemption. Suddenly the future looked like an endless progression of possibilities: "Because of the LORD's great love we are not consumed, for his compassions never fail. They are new every morning; great is your faithfulness" (verses 22–23).

What hope and encouragement do you find in the prophet's change of heart? What do you think caused this change?

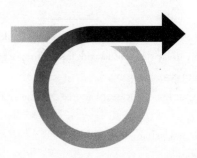

As you look at the Starting Over Loop, what are your initial thoughts?

Which do you think is the most difficult step in the Starting Over Loop? What about that step makes it difficult?

How would your life look different if you could consistently practice the Starting Over Loop with your regrets?

Bringing It Home

What are some common excuses that keep us from walking through the Starting Over Loop?

What steps do you need to take in order to make the Starting Over Loop a regular part of how you deal with life's deepest regrets?

CHAPTER 12. HOW TO HELP OTHERS START OVER

Breaking the Ice

What was one of the most unexpected acts of kindness someone has ever done for you?

Digging Deeper

In chapter 2, we took a close look at Peter's denials (see Luke 22:54–62). Peter was one of Jesus's closest followers, yet he denied even knowing Jesus, not once but three times. If Peter were your friend and he came to you after denying Jesus three times, how would you have responded?

What lessons did you learn from how Dave helped his friend, Matthew, escape the Sorry Cycle that could assist you as you help a friend struggling with deep regrets?

What impresses you most about how Jesus approached his friend and follower Peter after Peter had denied him three times? How can Jesus's approach with Peter give you insight in how to help a friend struggling with regrets?

In chapter 12, the authors state that there are two redemptive truths people need to know and believe in order to start over:
- You are loved by God.
- You have a purpose from God.

Which truth do you think people struggle most to believe when they are mired in regret? Why do you think that is?

Which of the verses listed under "Truths for Starting Over" would you be most likely to share with a friend who wants to learn to love his or her regrets?

Bringing It Home
Look at the people on your "Starting Over Prayer List." Which one of those people will you ask God to give you the opportunity to walk through the Starting Over Loop with?

How can these principles, addressed in chapter 12, provide insight for you as you help this person start over?
- Prayer helps others recognize regret.
- Friends help others release regret.
- God's truth helps others redeem regret.

NOTES

Preface

1. Eva Rafetseder and Josef Perner, "When the Alternative Would Have Been Better: Counterfactual Reasoning and the Emergence of Regret," *Cognition and Emotion* 26, no. 5 (2012): 800–19. www.uni-salzburg.at/fileadmin/oracle_file _imports/2045212.PDF.

Chapter 1: The Sorry Cycle

1. Regrets posted between June 22 and June 25, 2015, at Secretregrets.com. Reprinted with permission. For more real-life regrets like these, see the Secret Regrets series of books by Kevin Hansen.
2. Melanie Greenberg, "The Psychology of Regret," *Psychology Today,* May 2012, www.psychologytoday.com/blog/the-mindful-self-express/201205/the -psychology-regret.
3. Donald is not his real name. I have changed identifying details of this story to protect this individual's privacy. But the facts about his refusal to address his mistakes so that he could move on, preferring instead to stay stuck in regret, are sadly true. I grieve for Donald to this day.
4. "A Penitential Order: Rite One," *The (Online) Book of Common Prayer,* 320, www.bcponline.org/HE/penord1.html.
5. Catherine E. Seta and John J. Seta, "Regret in Pursuit of Change and Mainte-nance Goals," *Motivation and Emotion* 37, no. 1 (March 2013): 177–84.
6. John Greenleaf Whitter, "Maud Muller," Bartleby.com, www.bartleby.com/248 /217.html.
7. Romans 8:22–23.

Chapter 2: Love Your Regrets

1. This story is based on Luke 22:24–34, 54–62 and parallel passages in the other Gospels. I have interjected a little of my own imagination into this retelling to try

to bring out the drama of wrongdoing and regret that occurred between Peter and his Master in the high priest's courtyard.

2. See 2 Corinthians 7:8–11.

3. Giorgio Coricelli and others, "Regret and Its Avoidance: A Neuroimaging Study of Choice Behavior," *Nature Neuroscience* 8, no. 9 (September 2005): 1255–62.

4. Colleen Saffrey, Amy Summerville, and Neal J. Roese, "Praise for Regret: People Value Regret Above Other Negative Emotions," *Motivation and Emotion* 32, no. 1 (March 2008): 46–54.

5. Marcel Zeelenberg and Rik Pieters, "A Theory of Regret Regulation 1.0," *Journal of Consumer Psychology* 17, no. 1 (January 2007): 2935.

6. Kathryn Schulz, "Don't Regret Regret," TED, www.youtube.com/watch?v=ka 8L1YMR88U. Schulz is the author of *Being Wrong: Adventures in the Margin of Error.*

7. Steven C. Hayes and others, *Acceptance and Commitment Therapy: The Process and Practice of Mindful Change,* 2nd ed. (New York: Guilford, 2011), 64.

8. Not his real name, though the facts of his situation are all true to life.

9. Galatians 4:8–9.

10. See John 21 for the source of this fictionalized retelling of Peter's reinstatement by Jesus.

Chapter 3: Step #1: Recognize Your Regrets

1. JoJo Moyes and Marianne Macdonald, "Tragic Ending After Lottery Win That Wasn't," *The Independent* (UK), April 11, 1995, www.independent.co.uk/news /tragic-ending-after-lottery-win-that-wasnt-1615110.html; and Ian MacKinnon, "Lottery Loser Killed Himself for Just Pounds 27," *The Independent* (UK), June 16, 1995, www.independent.co.uk/news/lottery-loser-killed-himself-for-just -pounds-27-1586618.html.

2. Dallas Willard, "Transformation of the Mind," Summer 2003, www.dwillard .org/articles/artview.asp?artID=120.

3. 2 Corinthians 10:5.

4. *Gone with the Wind,* dir. Victor Fleming (Warner Brothers, 1940).

5. Stefania Bianchi and Mahmoud Habboush, "Wolf of Wall Street Belfort Is Aiming for $100 Million Pay," *Bloomberg,* May 19, 2014, www.bloomberg

.com/news/articles/2014-05-19/wolf-of-wall-street-belfort-sees-pay-top-100
-million-this-year.

6. Joel M. Cohen, "The Real Belfort Story Missing from 'Wolf' Movie," *New York Times,* January 7, 2014, http://dealbook.nytimes.com/2014/01/07/the-real -belfort-story-missing-from-wolf-movie/?_r=0.

7. This retelling is creatively based on 2 Samuel 11:1–12:23. The extended quote is from 2 Samuel 12:1–4.

8. Dave Ferguson and Jon Ferguson, *Finding Your Way Back to God: 5 Awakenings to Your New Life* (Colorado Springs, CO: Multnomah, 2015), 88–90. To hear Steve tell his story in his own words, go to YouTube and search for "Tough Times: Steve Ciambrone." You should find five video segments in which Steve gives his testimony.

9. 1 Peter 5:7.

Chapter 4: Step #2: Release Your Regrets

1. 2 Samuel 12:13.

2. See 1 Samuel 13:14.

3. See 1 Samuel 17:47.

4. See 2 Samuel 6:14–16.

5. 2 Samuel 23:1, NASB.

6. Psalm 51, preface.

7. Psalm 51:2–3.

8. Psalm 51:11–12.

9. 2 Samuel 12:13.

10. See 2 Samuel 12:14–23.

11. 1 John 1:9.

12. Joshua 4:1–9.

13. Names and identifying details in this story have been changed.

14. Romans 12:18, emphasis added.

15. Lewis B. Smedes, *Forgive and Forget: Healing the Hurts We Don't Deserve* (San Francisco: HarperOne, 1996), 131.

16. See Luke 23:34.

17. See Romans 5:10.

18. See Matthew 6:14–15 and 18:21–35.

19. Colossians 3:13.
20. Elahe Izadi, "The Powerful Words of Forgiveness Delivered to Dylann Roof by Victims' Relatives," *Washington Post,* June 19, 2015, www.washingtonpost.com /news/post-nation/wp/2015/06/19/hate-wont-win-the-powerful-words -delivered-to-dylann-roof-by-victims-relatives/.
21. See Matthew 5:44.

Chapter 5: Step #3: Redeem Your Regrets

1. "Origins of Rugby," Rugbyfootballhistory.com, 2007, www.rugbyfootballhistory .com/webb-ellis.html and www.rugbyfootballhistory.com/originsofrugby.htm.
2. Romans 8:28.
3. Adapted from Lynn Sweet, *Life on an Epic Scale,* 27–28.
4. See Luke 15:11–24.
5. See "My Story," Crissy Moran, http://newcrissymoran.com/bio/; and "The Restorer of My Heart, Mind, and Soul," *Crissy Moran* (blog), April 30, 2013, http://newcrissymoran.com/442/.
6. "Crissy's Story," *Treasures,* http://iamatreasure.com/stories/crissys-story/.
7. Names and identifying details in this story have been changed.
8. See Acts 16:25.
9. Isaiah 64:4.

Chapter 6: Finding Your Way Back

1. Jeremiah 29:13–14.
2. This version of the story is creatively based on Luke 15:11–32. For a much fuller treatment of this story, see our book *Finding Your Way Back to God.*
3. Russell Baker, *Growing Up* (1982; reprint, New York: Signet, 1992), 80–81.
4. John 14:6.
5. Luke 19:10.
6. See Matthew 20:1–16.

Chapter 7: Hearts at Risk

1. Mike Morrison and Neal J. Roese, "Regrets of the Typical American: Findings from a Nationally Representative Sample," *Social Psychological and Personality Science* 2, no. 6 (November 2011): 576–83.

2. Markku Jokisaari, "Regrets and Subjective Well-Being: A Life Course Approach," *Journal of Adult Development* 11, no. 4 (October 2004): 281–8.

3. Randi Gunther, quoted in Dave Singleton, "Men Reflect on Past Romantic Regrets," Match.com, www.match.com/magazine/article/12731/Men-Reflect-On-Past-Romantic-Regrets/.

4. The patriarchs' stories can be found in Genesis 12–50.

5. Names and identifying details in this story have been changed.

6. See Exodus 20:12, 14, 17.

7. See Ephesians 5:21–33.

8. See Colossians 3:21.

9. Creatively based on a family story that's well worth reading; see Genesis 41:41–47:12. The quoted verses are from Genesis 45:14–15.

10. Genesis 50:20; see also 45:5–8.

Chapter 8: Fit as Can Be

1. A. J. Jacobs, "How Healthy Living Nearly Killed Me," TED, October 2011, www.ted.com/talks/aj_jacobs_how_healthy_living_nearly_killed_me?language=e. See also A. J. Jacobs, *Drop Dead Healthy: One Man's Humble Quest for Bodily Perfection* (New York: Simon & Schuster, 2012).

2. 1 Corinthians 6:13.

3. See 2 Corinthians 5:1–4.

4. 1 Timothy 4:8.

5. 1 Corinthians 6:19.

6. 1 Corinthians 6:20.

7. Philippians 1:21–24.

8. Cited in Gretchen Reynolds, "The Benefits of Middle Age Fitness, *New York Times,* September 5, 2012, http://well.blogs.nytimes.com/2012/09/05/the-benefits-of-middle-age-fitness/?_r=0.

9. "Physical Activity and Health: Older Adults," Centers for Disease Control and Prevention, www.cdc.gov/nccdphp/sgr/pdf/olderad.pdf.

10. *The Lancet,* "Adults Who Lose Weight at Any Age Could Enjoy Improved Cardiovascular Health," *ScienceDaily,* May 20, 2014, www.sciencedaily.com/releases/2014/05/140520184801.htm.

11. "Stop Smoking Recovery Timetable," WhyQuit.com, http://whyquit.com/whyquit/A_Benefits_Time_Table.html.

12. Charles Duhigg, *The Power of Habit* (New York: Random House, 2012), 19.
13. John 11:25.
14. Psalm 92:14.

Chapter 9: Dollars and Sense

1. See Matthew 25:14–30.
2. Matthew 11:30.
3. "Steve Martin: Quotes," IMDB.com, http://m.imdb.com/name/nm0000188 /quotes.
4. National Foundation for Credit Counseling, press release, "NFCC Poll Reveals Consumers' Top Financial Regrets," PRWeb, July 2, 2012, www.prweb.com /releases/2012/7/prweb9663024.htm.
5. Brad Klontz and others, "Money Beliefs and Financial Behaviors: Development of the Klontz Money Script Inventory," *Journal of Financial Therapy* 2, no. 1 (2011).
6. Thomas, "Completely Debt FREE—House and All!" Dave Ramsey, September 2, 2015, www.daveramsey.com/articles/article-list/category/100424/story ID/104378.
7. Matthew 25:21, 23.

Chapter 10: My Why

1. Mike Morrison and Neal J. Roese, "Regrets of the Typical American: Findings from a Nationally Representative Sample," *Social Psychological and Personality Science* 2, no. 6 (November 2011): 576–83.
2. Statistic cited in "7 Questions to Finding Your True Passion," I Need Motivation, www.ineedmotivation.com/blog/2008/04/7-questions-to-finding-your-true -passion/.
3. See Acts 9:1–9.
4. Ephesians 2:10.
5. For the source of this retelling, see Exodus 2:11–3:2.
6. Philippians 2:13.
7. Ephesians 3:20.
8. Patrick L. Hill and Nicholas A. Turiano, "Purpose in Life as a Predictor of Mortality Across Adulthood," *Psychological Science* 25, no. 7 (July 2014): 1482–6.

9. Emily Esfahani Smith, "There's More to Life than Being Happy," *The Atlantic,* January 9, 2013, www.theatlantic.com/health/archive/2013/01/theres-more-to-life-than-being-happy/266805/.

10. John 19:30.

11. Colossians 1:20.

Chapter 11: Living Beyond Your Regrets

1. Lamentations 3:19–21.

2. Lamentations 3:22–23.

3. The names have been changed in this story.

4. See Mark 9:14–29.

5. Revelation 21:3–5.

Chapter 12: How to Help Others Start Over

1. Paraphrase of Luke 22:54–60.

2. John 21:15.

ABOUT THE AUTHORS

Dave Ferguson is founding and lead pastor of Chicago's Community Christian Church, a multisite missional community considered one of the most influential churches in America. Dave is also the visionary for NewThing, a global network of reproducing churches, and President of the Exponential Conference. Dave and his wife, Sue, have three children.

Jon Ferguson is founding pastor of Community Christian Church, a teaching pastor, and movement leader for NewThing. He and his wife, Lisa, have two children.

Brothers Dave and Jon are the coauthors of *Finding Your Way Back to God*.

"God, if you're real, make yourself real to me."

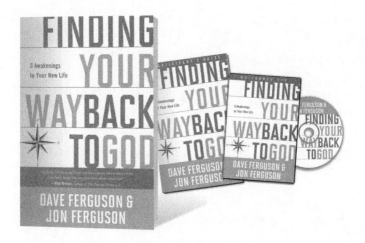

Finding Your Way Back to God puts you on the road of authentic spiritual discovery—starting wherever you are right now. Wake up to who you really are, and dare to believe that God wants to be found even more than you want to find him. He is ready to help you find your way back.

Five-session DVD & Participant's Guide also available separately.
Perfect for groups or individuals.

Start reading now at WaterBrookMultnomah.com!